WHY YOU ARE NOT ATTRACTING WHAT YOU WANT

11 MOST COMMON MISTAKES THAT YOU ARE LIKELY MAKING WHILE APPLYING THE LAW OF ATTRACTION

MIA HAMMOND

CONTENTS

INTRODUCTION

Ten years ago, my life was an absolute mess. I was broke and living in a shabby one bedroom apartment. My marriage of five years ended in a bitter divorce. I felt aimless and goalless. It was as if I was floating through life in whatever direction the tempestuous currents of daily living would take me. The word tempestuous may sound like an exaggeration, but that really is the only word I can use to describe what I was going through. Every day, life seemed to randomly throw a new curveball at me that I had no idea how to handle.

I felt miserable, despondent, and clueless about my very existence. Had I been born just to suffer and be miserable? The idea that there was a higher purpose to life seemed to completely elude me.

Are you in a similar situation? Do you feel things aren't working for you or at least aren't working the way you would like?

I urge you to take a deeper look at your mind and the thoughts you most frequently engage in. Do you focus on what you want or do you often find yourself thinking about what you don't want? How do you feel when you visualize yourself having exactly what you desire (if you are able to get yourself to visualize it)? Do you feel worthy and deserving of what you desire or, somewhere deep inside you, do you feel what you want is something impossible for you to attain?

What are you imagining right now? Are you imagining what may go wrong or are you imagining the successful fulfillment of your goals and desires? What kind of thoughts are coming up in your mind right now?

The thing with life is that we don't get what we want; we get what we think about, or feel, the most. There is no such thing as luck. We are the creators of our own destiny. Wherever we focus our energy becomes our reality. If you honestly answered the questions above, I am sure you are starting to observe that you don't think enough about what you want; you are almost always thinking about what you don't want. Therefore, you are always getting what you are not hoping to receive.

There are no exceptions when it comes to how the law of the Universe works. What we sow, we must reap. No one can cheat the law; it works every single time in exactly the same way for every human being on the planet.

Coming back to my story, I did manage to turn my life around. The transformation started only when I began taking full responsibility for my life, when I realized I was the only person responsible for how my life had panned out.

Now, this idea makes most people defensive. They question how they are responsible for all the bad things that other people have done to them. You must understand one thing: taking responsibility doesn't imply accepting blame. I'm not asking you to blame yourself for all the negative things that others have done to you. Far from it; I am suggesting that you start taking responsibility for the fact that every experience of life is, at some level, the creation of our subconscious mind, whether we consciously ask for it or not. We always receive exactly what we deserve, even if it's not aligned to what we want or expect.

I know this isn't easy to accept, but when I started fully

embracing this idea, my life turned around completely. I started treating people how I wanted to be treated, and people changed toward me; they started treating me differently, too. In several cases, someone who had been terribly nasty toward me in the past suddenly changed completely, becoming kinder and more positive toward me. In other cases, the people who didn't have my best interest at heart simply disappeared from my radar. It's interesting how it all happened on its own quite rapidly.

I can't guarantee that the people who haven't been good to you will suddenly change their behavior toward you. That may or may not happen. But what I can guarantee is you will start attracting more positive people into your life, and the old dysfunctional relationships will either fall apart completely or will no longer bother you.

For me, taking responsibility meant that if I had unwittingly created a life I did not like, I could intentionally create the kind of life I have always wanted to live. It is entirely in my own hands. The power of choice is completely mine!

One thing led to another as I started understanding and practicing the law of attraction. Every aspect of my life changed once I began clearly defining what I wanted and applying the law of attraction to achieve the goals I had set for myself. It wasn't easy, and I had to overcome a lot of limitations to get to the point where I started seeing significant results, but it did happen quite rapidly.

Also, the results I manifested motivated me to continue doing the work. Soon there was a snowball effect on every aspect of my life. Over time, everything changed. I manifested a beautiful marriage with the man of my dreams. Now, I am enjoying a blissful family life with my husband and amazing child. Every morning, I wake up motivated and excited to spend another day doing exactly what I love doing. My career path is now fully aligned with my life purpose.

If I can have these results, then so can you! You can have everything you desire. The life of your dreams is already within your reach. In this book, I will show you exactly how you can apply the law of attraction to create the life you have always wanted to live.

This book has 11 chapters. The number 11 has a special significance in numerology. It indicates spiritual awakening and the ability to transcend all limitations. My intention for you is that by absorbing the wisdom of these 11 chapters and implementing it in your life, you may transcend all limitations to manifest the life you have always dreamed of.

So, without further ado, let's get started on this exciting journey!

CHAPTER 1

IS THE LAW OF ATTRACTION AN ABSOLUTE LAW?

> Thoughts become things. If you see it in your mind, you will hold it in your hand.

BOB PROCTOR (YOU WERE BORN RICH, 1997)

Since this book is about why the law of attraction is not working for you, I assume that you already know what the law of attraction is. However, for the benefit of those just starting out with it, I'll devote a chapter to explain exactly what the law of attraction is, how it works, and the correct process for manifesting anything you desire.

This book isn't purely theoretical or a rehash of other people's teachings. I am writing this book based on my own experiences over more than a decade. I would say I am an advanced manifester. I am at a point in life where things manifest really quickly for me. However, I didn't get here in a day or two. It took a lot of research, experimentation, patience, and attitude and habit shifts to get here. I am writing this book to make the process much quicker for you.

I have advanced knowledge and understanding of the law of attraction. I'm not saying this to boast but simply to give you the reassurance that you are in safe and experienced hands. I understand what it feels like to be frustrated when you think you are doing everything right—at least the way a certain famous book told you to do—but to not get the results. What could you possibly be doing wrong and, more importantly, how do you make it work for you?

I am here to answer all those questions, but in this chapter, I want to share with you the best and most advanced manifesting techniques that you can use to create just about anything you like. These techniques are based on the teachings of an exemplary spiritual teacher, Neville Goddard. They are far more detailed, descriptive, and advanced than what most people in this niche share. I have used these techniques to manifest the marriage of my dreams, a career that is fully aligned with my life path, and innumerable other blessings.

WHAT IS THE LAW OF ATTRACTION?

The entire Universe is governed by certain absolute laws. They cannot be negotiated, altered or changed. They work even when we aren't aware of them. For instance, one of the absolute laws on our planet is the law of gravity. Now, you can't jump from a five story building and say, "I don't believe in gravity." You can choose to willfully ignore the law of gravity, but that doesn't mean it doesn't affect you. The same is true for the law of attraction.

It is important to understand that when we talk about the law of attraction, we imply that we are using it intentionally. The law is always working whether you are using it consciously in your favor or not. Every single thing you have or are experiencing right now is a creation. You are the creator of your world and of every single life experience you have ever had. I know this can be a hard pill to swallow but the key to your freedom and empowerment lies in embracing this truth fully.

I'm not suggesting that you slip into guilt. I'm saying that if you have created circumstances you don't desire, then you also have the power to create circumstances that you do desire. But you can't claim your power if you continue to believe that something outside of you is running the show for you. You are the architect of your destiny, the writer and director of your life's movie.

Just like a movie script, you can write anything to your life script, and eventually it will manifest. You have always been manifesting; even right now you are manifesting. Nothing in life is a coincidence; everything is a creation and a manifestation. You have manifested this book into your life. I am sure you have felt lately that you really want things to change. You are ready for something bigger and better. You want to get the law of attraction working for you. As is always the case, the Universe heard your appeal and sent this book your way.

For a moment, close your eyes and think about the way in which you found this book. What prompted you to pick it up? Was it a hunch—a powerful sense of intuition—that maybe this is where you will find the answers you have been desperately looking for? Perhaps someone gifted you this book and you felt compelled to open it to get to this page.

Intuition is the secret language through which the Universe constantly communicates with us. We are never alone because we are one with the Universe. The Universe is within you, and the Universe is you. There is nothing outside. Everything you are seeking is within you. You don't need to desperately chase success in the world. You simply need to sit back, relax, and trust that what you want is already yours. If you can get yourself into such a state, the Universe will guide you through your intuition to take inspired action. That's how you will succeed in every venture.

DOES THE LAW OF ATTRACTION WORK EVERY SINGLE TIME?

Even though I have already stated that the law of attraction is an absolute law, you are probably still wondering if it works EVERY SINGLE TIME or if there are some exceptions to its application. After all, if you are struggling with your manifestations, then maybe there are special cases where the law doesn't apply. That's what you are thinking, isn't it?

Let me be very clear: there are absolutely no exceptions to the law of attraction. It is ALWAYS working. If you are not getting the results you desire, that doesn't mean you are lacking the capability to manifest. We have all been endowed with the same power to manifest. The law of attraction is a universal law that works equally for all of us. It never goes on a hiatus; consciously or unconsciously, we are always manifesting.

Now, the question is why does it feel like it's not working for you? Trust me, what you want is already yours! You simply have to remove all the blockages that prevent you from claiming it right now. How will you do it? That's exactly what this book is here to help you figure out. If you'll do all the exercises and implement all the teachings I share in this book, then your life will change for the better. It will happen so miraculously and surprisingly fast that you will be amazed.

EXERCISE

I will now share a powerful exercise with you. I have myself been doing this for the last decade. This exercise will reinforce your belief in the law of attraction. You'll realize for yourself that the law of attraction is always working no matter what.

Every morning, create a list of ten small things you want to manifest. These should be things that don't mean much to you or that you are okay with not manifesting. Write everything in the present tense. For instance, the list can be something like: I am receiving a compliment; I am receiving a cup of free coffee; I am receiving $10; I have red flowers in the house.

Every couple of days, go through the lists you have created and keep striking off everything that has manifested. You will be absolutely amazed by how many items you get to check off your list. Do it and see for yourself!

Just keep in mind, this exercise is meant to help you develop your faith in the universality and potency of the law of attraction. Don't pick big things that mean a lot to you, or you will start feeling obsessive about it. You will realize that things manifest very quickly when you are relaxed about what you want to manifest.

SO CAN YOU REALLY ATTRACT EVERYTHING YOU DESIRE?

Absolutely, yes! Nothing is too big or too small for the Universe. The only limitations are the ones you impose upon yourself.

In reality, everything is energy. It doesn't matter whether you want to manifest a million dollars or ten dollars. They are both made out of the same energetic fabric. It doesn't take any more work on the part of the Universe to bring you a million dollars or any less work to get you ten dollars. They are both different manifestations of the energy of money.

I know most people associate money with materialism. But that's far from the truth. Money is a form of energy like everything else in the entire Universe. Material and spiritual life are two sides of the same coin. You can't manifest anything in the material world without mastering the law of attraction and attaining a certain level of spiritual mastery over yourself. Spiritual growth may feel incomplete without material success. Hence, you must aspire for both if you want to live a full and wholesome life.

There's absolutely nothing in this world you can't have, become, or attract. It doesn't matter what your past has been; from this point onward, you can live your life fully on your own terms. If you can simply believe you can have something and you convince yourself that you already have it, then there is no force in the entire Universe that can prevent you from getting what you want.

STEP-BY-STEP INSTRUCTIONS FOR MANIFESTING ANYTHING YOU WANT

Many of the popular law of attraction gurus talk a lot about what the law of attraction is and how it works, but they never provide any clear step-by-step instructions for using it. If you are anything like me, you want a clear process you can follow each time instead of trying to blindly shoot an arrow in the ether.

Besides, the law of attraction is a science. Manifestation is a highly scientific process. If you follow all the steps, then you'll definitely receive your manifestation. It will happen in its own time, just like each seed has its own germination period after which it sprouts into a plant.

So, here's how you'd do it:

1. Decide Exactly What You Want

If you wanted to go on a trip, would you just sit in your car and start driving without a sense of direction or any idea of a destination? Obviously not.

The problem is that most people don't know exactly what they want. In fact, I can assure you that most people fail at manifestation simply because they aren't clear about exactly what they want. We'll delve more deeply into that in the next chapter. For now, I want you to understand that to be successful at manifesting, you must have a very clear idea of exactly what it is you want to manifest. There's no room for being vague or wishy-washy about it.

You must know what you want in as much detail and specificity as possible. If you want to go on a vacation, then you research a destination. Thereafter, you find out the best mode of transport to get there. Perhaps you research flight tickets and book your seats with the airline of your choice. You also make your hotel reservations and then start packing to leave on the finalized date.

Manifesting isn't that much different from planning a vacation. You must decide your destination by setting a clear goal for what you want. You must then take all the steps I will outline here. These steps are as crucial for successful manifestation as booking your tickets and reserving your place at the hotel when you go on a vacation.

If you aren't 100% sure about what you want, do not despair. I'll help you develop greater clarity on it. For now, let's do a simple exercise.

EXERCISE

Imagine that the Universe is your very own Santa Claus and you are a child on Christmas morning. As a child who hasn't been programmed by society and family yet, you believe everything is possible. You can be whoever you want to be and have whatever you want to have. There are no limitations; you can have absolutely anything you wish for.

Now, write down exactly what comes to mind right now. What is it that you truly want? I'm not talking about what you believe you can have or what you think is possible for you to have. Think freely, as if all your limitations have dropped off your consciousness like excess baggage and you are ready to soar high like an eagle.

Write down what you want. Do it right now. Don't put it off. Don't just settle for thinking about it. You must put it on paper right now. I forbid you to read any further until you have completed this task. I know that sounds a bit harsh, but you'll thank me for it. I can promise you that!

Don't worry if you aren't entirely sure about what you want right now. The more you think about it, the clearer it will become.

Over time, you can modify and refine your goals. The next chapter will help you gain a lot of clarity. For now, just get started and work on developing the habit of setting goals. You get what you want in life only when you know what it is you are aspiring for.

2. Create an Imaginal Act

Your imagination is the tool through which you can create anything you desire. It's like the Universe has blessed you with all the raw ingredients you need to craft your favorite dish. Now, you can make a trashy fast-food burger or a gourmet Michelin meal. Your faculties of imagination work just as effectively for both. So do yourself a favor and aim high. Dream big!

Now, how do you create an imaginal act? Here are the steps:

Step 1: Close your eyes and visualize that you have already achieved your goal. You are the person you want to be, you have what you desire, and you are living your dream life. Take your time and visualize this in great detail.

Step 2: Now, pick something that would happen immediately after your wish has been fulfilled. For example, if you want to get married, you can create a scene where you are both lying in bed next to each other reflecting back on the beautiful wedding you had. You are also feeling, touching, and looking at the wedding rings that are now there on your fingers. Your partner says "I love you" and then you kiss.

In another example, let's say you want an expensive coat you saw at the store. The coat is just not in your budget, and it seems impossible that you'll ever be able to afford it. Fret not! As I told you earlier, there is nothing impossible for the Universe. If you can successfully see yourself having something in your imagination, then the Universe must bend over backward to give you your desire. It just can't be any other way! So now, create a scene where you are wearing the coat. You can feel how soft and luxurious the fabric is. You feel amazing in it. A friend of yours comes to you and compliments you on how much the coat suits you.

As you can see, there are two key aspects to creating a powerful imaginal act. One is to add as much tactile detail as possible to an event that takes place immediately after your goal has been fulfilled. Within the scene, there is a climactic moment that seals the deal. For example, in the first instance, it is the kiss. In the second one, it is the compliment.

So now, before reading forward, create a scene that represents the fulfillment of your desire.

3. Replay the Imaginal Act Every Morning and Night

For every person, the two most important times of the day are early in the morning immediately after waking up and right before bed when you are ready to go to sleep. At these hours, the doorways of the subconscious remain wide open. Whatever mental and emotional diet you are consuming at these two times finds its way into the deepest crevices and trenches of your subconscious.

If you spend your early morning and late night hours watching trash TV, then trash is what will manifest in your reality. In today's society, most people have become extremely callous with their diet. Their physical diets are just as bad as their mental and emotional diets. People thrive on gossip, drama, and negativity. They abuse their body with junk food and then wonder why nothing is working in their life. Do you see the irony?

If you want to become good at manifesting, then you must make better use of your early morning and late-night hours. To be successful in life, you must be intentional and disciplined with your time. From now on, right after you wake up and immediately before you retire for the night, start visualizing the imaginal act as if you were living in it. It is very important that you visualize every-thing from a first person perspective because that is how you are living in your reality right now. You don't see yourself in a movie on a screen. You are inside your body. You experience the world from inside your body. This is the perspective you must use during your visualization.

Keep playing the scene on repeat until you fall asleep. Saturate the scene with all the details of reality. Observe what you are wearing, what kind of colors and textures you see around; the point is to use all your five senses to feel the situation as completely real.

When you get to the climactic moment, like the kiss or the compliment, allow yourself to become fully saturated with the scene as if you were living it right now. Become one with the state of the wish fulfilled. You already have what you desire.

4. Drop the Desire

People often ask me if they need to remain in the state of the wish fulfilled all day. My answer is absolutely not. I tried doing that as well in my early days of manifesting. I thought if I lost the feeling of having my desire even for a few minutes or hours in a day, my manifestation would never come to pass.

This kind of attitude simply reinforces the lack of what you desire. You get frustrated, worried, impatient, and angry because your reality is constantly confirming you don't have what you desire.

It's important to note that the doors of the subconscious don't remain wide open throughout the day. Hence, not everything you think or feel will slip into your subconscious mind. When you get a negative thought, simply observe it and let it pass. Ask yourself this question, "Is there any evidence that it will manifest?" The answer is no.

What is better to believe? That you will get what you want or that you won't get what you want? I'd vote for the former. If you can train yourself to ask this question every time a negative thought arises, then you can overcome them very easily.

But if you are not able to let go of all your negative thoughts and limiting beliefs, it's okay! As long as you're doing the morning and night visualizations the way I laid out above, you will definitely get the results. Negative thinking may delay it for a bit, but it will eventually come to pass. You just have to remain consistent with how you are spending these two times of the day.

It is also very important to let go of the desire at some point, as holding on to it too tightly by constantly obsessing over it will only delay the manifestation. It's like a letter that you don't send. You have to do the visualization and then just get busy living your most amazing life possible!

5. Get Busy Living

I can't emphasize this enough! Don't put your life on hold until your wish is fulfilled. You must keep yourself in a high vibrational state by focusing on being happy and content. I am sure you remember times in your life when you badly wanted something that kept eluding you until you got busy doing other things and forgot about it. Something miraculous happened: you got what you wanted at a time when you were least expecting it!

Two things happened here. Firstly, you stopped being obsessed with your desire. The energy of obsession is the same as the energy of lack. When you are obsessed with trying to get something, you are constantly reinforcing the idea that you don't already have it. Secondly, when you are busy living a good life, you are in a high vibrational state. This automatically attracts all the good things you desire. You become extremely magnetic to the life, situations, and things you wish.

EXERCISE

Create a list of things you want to do but have never tried. Note down everything that comes to mind. It doesn't matter whether some of the things seem probable or practical at this time or not.

You don't want to miss out on any of your heart's true desires. If you truly want something, then the Universe will eventually find a way to give it to you.

Every time you get obsessive or negative thoughts, pick something from this list that you can do right now and get busy doing it. If you always wanted to sign up for that yoga class, then get subscribed for the trial today! If you want to start painting, then go to the store and buy the supplies you need; just get started RIGHT NOW! You'll be absolutely amazed by how this one simple exercise can change your life. Don't take it lightly; doing something you enjoy instantly puts you in a high vibrational state, which makes you magnetic to everything you desire.

CHAPTER 2

NOT BEING CLEAR ABOUT
WHAT YOU WANT

Set your mind on a definite goal and observe how quickly the world stands aside to let you pass.

NAPOLEON HILL (THINK AND GROW RICH, 2005)

You can't reach your destination without first knowing with total clarity exactly where you are headed. Think about it... You don't get in your car and drive in a random direction. You get in your car when you intend to go somewhere. You have a clear idea about your destination, and you start the journey with at least a rough idea of how you will get there. Isn't it odd that most people are steering through the alleys of life without any aim to reach a particular destination?

People complain about how bad things are for them. They want to have a different life, but if you ask most people exactly what it is they want, they stare at you with a blank face. Most people spend way too much time thinking about what they don't want while not giving enough thought to assessing what they do want. Can you relate to that?

Your thoughts shape your reality, even at this very moment. Everything you have and all that you experience is a result of your thoughts. Your reality constantly mirrors the belief system you hold inside at the deepest most fundamental level. The Universe doesn't distinguish between positive and negative thinking. It will never say, "Don't ask for it; it won't be good for you."

The Universe always gives you exactly what you ask for, which is what you always think about. If you are always focused on and complaining about all the bad things that happened to you in the past, it's likely more bad things will manifest in your reality. Similarly, if you are constantly worried about future events, guess what you'll be attracting? It's not what you desire that you get but what you currently think about, whether it's something you desire or not. In other words, you get what you truly expect to receive, even if you expect the worst.

If you are going on a trip and want to safely reach your destination, but you are constantly thinking about everything that can go wrong during the journey, what do you think you will attract to your experience? You will obviously attract undesirable experiences.

Most people complain and get angry at the Universe or blame their destiny for what they experience. However, you are the only person who is in charge of your destiny. You can shape it however you like by molding your thoughts to correspond with the reality that you want.

WHAT ARE YOU THINKING ABOUT RIGHT NOW?

Self-awareness is the master key to the gates of personal transformation. You can't change anything without first becoming aware of where you are at this moment. So, pause for a moment, close your eyes, and observe your thoughts.

What are you thinking about right now? Is it something positive or negative? Are you thinking about what you truly want to experience, or are you mulling over the possibility of undesirable events? If you are like most people, then you are currently thinking about everything you don't want. You are struggling to not obsess over the possibility of bad things happening. I must say, it is okay to have these kinds of thoughts!

We have developed these patterns of thinking through years of unconscious conditioning. Our parents, family, teachers, and other well-wishers want the best for us, but since they don't know any better themselves, they end up passing on their limited ways of thinking to us. The patterns of thoughts you find yourself engaging in weren't developed in a day. It takes a long time for thought patterns to become deeply embedded in your psyche. Hence, they can't also be undone in a day. You have to be persistent in your efforts to transform them.

Self-awareness is the first step in this process of transformation. Things start changing the very moment you become aware of things you would rather change. People who live in denial about their current reality can't experience transformation. They lack the courage to see things for what they are in the moment. Just like you can't drive from Houston to Washington if you don't first accept that your starting point is Houston, you can't start your journey of personal transformation without fully accepting all the thoughts that you constantly engage in—the good and the bad; the positive and the negative. You have to accept and embrace the full spectrum of thoughts and the emotions that accompany them.

HOW TO DEVELOP CLARITY ABOUT WHAT YOU TRULY WANT

Although it contradicts what I've just been talking about, if you have no idea what you truly want, you can start by thinking about what you know for sure you don't want. What we want is often the exact opposite of what we fear and think about. Jack Canfield famously said, "everything you want is on the other side of fear" (Goodreads, n.d.). This is not an exaggerated statement by any means. Analyzing what you fear and what you don't want can give you critical clues to uncover what you do want.

So, ask yourself the following questions:

- What do I find myself obsessively thinking about?
- Do I spend most of my time thinking about what I want or about what I don't want?
- If I am thinking about what I don't want, what is the exact opposite? Would that give me the happiness and satisfaction I crave deep down?

Don't ask yourself these questions just mentally; to develop complete clarity, you must write the answers down. Once you have everything written down, you can create a counter story that resonates with what you truly want.

For instance, if you are constantly worried you won't have enough money for your needs or you find yourself resorting to a lot of fear-based behavior around money, you can create a new story in which you always have more money than you need. In this story, you affirm to yourself that it is easy for you to live a comfortable and luxurious life where all your needs are easily met. Use the principles that I shared in the previous chapter to create a scene of *living in the end*—the point where you already have what you want right now.

THE MORE PRECISE YOU ARE, THE BETTER IT IS

People often have a rough idea of what they want but are not specific enough to communicate it to the Universe. For instance, a lot of people say they want to be rich, but they don't have a clear idea about what being rich means to them. Since this is a relative term, there is no one-size-fits-all; being rich can mean completely different things to different people.

So, if it is money you want to attract and manifest into your life (and who doesn't want that?), then you must start by asking yourself exactly how much money it would take for you to afford the kind of lifestyle you desire. To get a realistic idea, you can research the lives of people who already live the way you want to live. If you can get down to a very specific number, then your chances of getting what you want skyrocket.

Doing ample research prior to setting the scene for *living in the end* and replaying it every night is essential for sending a clear message to the Universe. It's like placing an order at a restaurant. If you're vague, then your chances of receiving what you want are slim. For instance, imagine telling the waiter, "Please bring me something that is warm and soft." An order like that would confuse the waiter. He would try his best to give you exactly what you have requested, but there are far too many dishes that meet your criteria. However, since he can bring you only one or two dishes at a time, it's unlikely you would like what he serves you.

Obviously, you don't place an order in such a manner. You specify the name of the dish and then you put down the menu. You know the waiter will bring you what you ordered. It works the same way with the Universe. You need to know exactly what you want to order and then you need to relax and let go, trusting the Universe to deliver your order at the best time.

You don't peek into the restaurant's kitchen to check whether the chef is preparing your order or not. You don't constantly ask the waiter if he has really taken your order or not. You simply relax and trust that you'll be served at the right moment. It's the same for manifesting what you desire. The Universe is your waiter, always ready to serve you whatever you desire. Your imagination is your menu and order board. What you imagine becomes yours!

EXERCISE

Analyze your thoughts to see what you think about most of the time. Replace all unwanted thoughts with positive uplifting ones. Create an imaginal act that reinforces the idea of having already received what you desire (refer to the directions laid out in Chapter 1).

Make your imaginal acts as precise and specific as possible. You don't have to know every single detail, but you definitely need to get all the important details on point. So, if you want to get married, it's not enough to say you want a good man. You want to define what a good man is to you, along with the nature of the relationship you want to have with him. Do ample research and make sure you have all the important points down to make your imaginal act as real and detailed as possible.

CHAPTER 3
REMAINING STUCK IN THE PAST

66 I have realized that the past and future are real illu-
sions, that they exist in the present, which is what
there is and all there is.

ALAN WILSON WATTS (GOODREADS, N.D.)

Most people won't ever get the chance to live the life of
their dreams because they allow their past to influence their present and dictate their future. I am sure
you have heard the saying that time is only an illusion. While it
sounds like a grand concept worth appreciating, few of us understand the true meaning behind it.

Let's try something: think about something good that has
happened to you in the past. Are you imagining it? Are you able to
feel the emotions that this memory is evoking in you?

Now, think about a negative past event. Are you able to imagine
it as vividly as if it were happening with you right now? Does it
evoke strong emotions in you so it feels like you are undergoing it
all over again?

Whether it is a good memory that you cherish or a negative

memory that fills you with difficult emotions, you can't experience either by going into the past. You relive, recall, and re-experience it only by bringing it into the present. Hence, the past is an illusion, as you can't recall the past without revoking and reinstating it in the present.

No matter how good or bad the past was, it no longer exists. The only place where it continues to live on is within your mind and your memory. By altering your perception of the past, you can transform your relationship with it. Once you have altered your relationship with the past, turning it into a more positive and pleasant one, it can no longer impact or influence your current reality.

No matter how bad things have been in the past, they have no need to affect your current reality and the future you want to create. It really doesn't matter where you are coming from; the only thing that matters is where you want to go. You can have, be, and do anything you wish to have, be, and do. You are only limited by your imagination and what you believe is possible.

ALTER THE PAST

Most people believe that the past cannot be altered. It has been done and nothing can undo what has already been done. I am here to tell you something different. If the past is only an illusion and exists only in the present, then you can turn it into anything you wish it to be. Just because you made a mistake or missed an important opportunity, it doesn't mean you have to live with the emotional consequences of it forever. You can change the past today and completely alter your destiny right now.

Perhaps that sounds too good to be true: How can anyone change the past? I'm not asking you to take my word for it. I will now share with you a scientific systematic method through which you can alter any past event. It's not something that works at random.

This method works every single time without fail because it is based on the laws of the Universe. This method derives from the work of Neville Goddard (The Neville Collection: All 10 Books by a Modern Master, 2020). I have used it many times to change my perception of past and current events. The method is called "revision" and can also be used to revise or redo experiences of daily life that didn't turn out the way you would have liked.

EXERCISE

Create a list of all the events from the past that didn't pan out the way you would have liked. Be sure to include anything and everything that bothers you to this day. No incident is too small or too big for revision. You don't have to believe right now that something can be done about these incidents. Just create a list of all the events you wish had panned out differently.

HOW TO REVISE THE PAST

Please complete the exercise above before continuing, as it's important for you to know exactly which incident you want to change or alter before you start the process. If you have too many such incidents on your list, start by picking out one that bothers you the most. Don't worry if logic tells you it cannot be revised. All things are possible for the Universe. If something is bothering you, then you have the power to change the incident and how it affects you.

Once you have made a note of the event you wish had played out differently, get yourself into a state of deep relaxation and allow yourself to relive the moments that led to the unwanted event. Relive the experience until the last few moments before the event took place and stop there. From that point on, create a different story. Visualize the way you wish things had unfolded.

Fill this new version with all the tones of reality you can add. Keep yourself in a deeply relaxed state akin to sleep and continue replaying this new revised version of events in your mind. Do this until you fall asleep for several nights in a row. There is no specific recommendation for how many times you should do it to be sure that the revised version of the event is now in full effect. If you can do it properly even just once, the revision has happened. Your reality will eventually conform with this new revised version of the past. you will be amazed by how the Universe brings this about, which often occurs in the most unexpected of ways.

After a few days, when you feel you have really saturated yourself with all the feelings and emotions that this new revised event evokes in you, you can drop the manifestation and move on. Don't mull over how things should or would happen or what the Universe will do to support your manifestation. Manifestations often come about when we least expect them. Our attachment and obsessive thinking about the things we are trying to manifest can delay our desires from showing up in our reality. Hence, dropping the desire and moving on to other things is an essential component of the manifestation process.

Moving forward, whenever you are reminded of the unwanted event and how it unfolded, evoke this revised version of the incident and focus all your energy on it. Infuse it with all the tones of reality so it begins to feel completely real.

Neville Goddard recommends that we revise the events of each day before we go to sleep. This way, we won't accumulate a stock of unwanted events and memories. We can wipe the board of all unwanted events and replace them with whatever it is we want.

I know you must be a bit suspicious about how revision will work. It took me a while to come to terms with it, as well, when I learned about it initially. I'm not expecting you to do this with complete faith right now, but just give it a try! In the next section, I will share some stories with you that will bolster your faith in revision and may even inspire you to try to revise events that you would otherwise dismiss as impossible to alter.

USE THE POWER OF REVISION TO REMOVE ALL REGRETS

The amazing thing about revision is that it is not limited to modifying unwanted events. You can also use the power of revision to go back and do things you wish you had done. For instance, I really regretted missing the chance to have invested in some stocks. If I had made the investment, I would have profited in the present.

I went back into the past and revised how things had panned out, changing the fact that instead of living with the regret of not having made the investment, I had actually invested in the stocks. I followed the process of revision that I laid down in the previous exercise.

Something absolutely incredible happened. Out of nowhere, I received the exact amount of money that I would have made had I actually invested in the stocks. As I said earlier, the Universe always finds a way to bring to you exactly what you expect to receive. It doesn't matter at which point in time you try to manifest your desires; the past, the present, and the future exist simultaneously. This present moment in the here and now is the only thing that is real.

INSPIRING STORIES OF REVISION

If you are anything like me, you want to see proof that revision works. Sure, it's great that I've told you the past can be revised, but is there anyone who has successfully done it? I will now share with you some of my own personal stories and the stories of my family and friends who have used the law of attraction in their life to get what they want. Of course, all names and identifying details have been changed to protect everyone's privacy.

RELIEF FROM CHRONIC BACK PAIN

A friend of mine has been a professional athlete for more than a decade. He had suffered from chronic back pain for at least five years. When I shared the technique of revision with him, he decided to give it a try. He went back in time to the game he had played after which his back issues began. He visualized a different outcome and saturated the new revised version of events with all the hues of reality.

Nothing happened for a week or two, but he persisted in his efforts. Every night, he fell asleep visualizing the version of events he wished he had experienced. Around the third week, something miraculous happened. He woke up and was free of back pain. There was no trace of it, and the back pain never returned. Believe it or not, you can use revision to heal physical injuries, diseases, and other such issues.

THE MOST INCREDIBLE STORY I HAVE EVER ENCOUNTERED

One of my very close friends wasn't truly convinced that revision is something real. But out of sheer curiosity, she decided to give it a try. She figured since she was willing to experiment, then why not pick the most seemingly impossible event to revise.

Hence, she decided to undo the death of her dog who had tragically passed away in a car accident. It had been a terrible blow from which she had never recovered. She had trouble shaking off the trauma of losing her favorite pet who had been with her for a very long time.

She went back in time and revised the scene where the accident took place. In this new scene, the dog escaped being crushed by the car and came back home safely. She played the incident over and over in her mind for a few days and then totally forgot about it. Of course, she wasn't expecting anything out of this, so that made the process of dropping the desire even easier.

After a few days, something absolutely incredible happened. Her husband came home with a dog that resembled her old dog so closely that she felt it was him. He told her that he had found the dog wandering about their yard that evening. The dog looked emaciated, so there was a strong likelihood that he had been abandoned or he had gotten lost.

She and her husband agreed to publish an advertisement in the newspaper, and if no one came to claim him, they would keep him. The ad was published, but no one ever came. She knew from the moment she saw that dog, that he was hers. It's really amazing the incredible ways in which the Universe bends over backward to give us what we want. We don't know exactly how revision would play out, but it works without fail every single time!

A BROKEN RELATIONSHIP WAS HEALED

I had a major fallout with my best friend several years ago. We hadn't spoken to each other in ages. I regretted how things had played out, but I no longer had her contact details to connect with her and apologize.

I decided to go back in time and rewrite the incident that led to the fight we had had. I revised the past in such a way that it would completely erase all memories of the fight. I fell asleep visualizing this new revised version of events and continued the process for several days.

After a while, I got busy with life and totally forgot about this. A few weeks later, I was at a bookstore, and there she was! She quickly recognized me, and we both couldn't contain our excitement at having randomly bumped into each other. She apologized for the things she hadn't done right when we had that fallout, and I apologized sincerely for my own mistakes.

We talked for hours that day as if no time had passed. Since then, our relationship has been stronger and even more beautiful than we had ever imagined possible.

I never thought this is how my revision would pan out in the present. However, keep in mind that if you are in a similar situation, you will not necessarily have the exact same experience. The Universe may bring you a completely different solution to your regret, but trust me, revision ALWAYS works! You simply need to let go of your need to control everything. Your job is to simply visualize what you want; the Universe will figure out the way to give you what you truly desire.

KEEP YOURSELF ROOTED IN THE PRESENT

You can only change things in the present moment. Your power lies in the here and now. Even if you want to alter the past, you can transform it only by reliving and revising it in the present. The present moment is the only powerful moment. By constantly mulling over the past, you give your power away.

You can manifest anything you want; there are absolutely no limits to what's possible. But for this, you must keep yourself rooted in the present. You must also accept the present moment for exactly what it is. Indeed, there will be things you don't like within your current reality, but you must take full responsibility for every aspect of your life. By taking full responsibility, I don't imply feeling guilty or blaming yourself for things. Taking full responsibility is more about recognizing the fact that if you can create undesirable circumstances, events, and things, then you are also powerful enough to create whatever you want.

To remain connected with your true power at all times, try your best to keep your mind and your consciousness in the present.

EXERCISE

The best way to get yourself fully present in the here and now is to focus on your breath. Your breath is your connection to the Universe. The moment you start to focus on your breath, you immediately re-establish your connection with the powerful forces of the Universe.

Here's a simple practice you can do anytime, anywhere. You don't need any special equipment to practice it, and you can practice it as often as you wish. In fact, the more frequently you do so, the more it becomes ingrained into your system.

With each inhalation, observe how your breath enters your nose and lungs and how it spreads inside your body, infusing every part of you with renewed energy and vitality. With each exhalation, visualize all your tensions, stresses, worries, and negative emotions leaving your body. Your body will become fully relaxed. As you take in each breath and as you exhale each breath, count to four. 1-2-3-4 inhale. 1-2-3-4 exhale.

This may seem like a simple exercise, but it is an effective method for bringing your mind and your consciousness to the present. Your goal should be to keep yourself rooted in the present at all times. Whenever your mind begins to wander, use this breathing exercise to bring yourself back into the present moment.

CHAPTER 4
MANIFESTING IN THE FUTURE

66 The past, the present and the future are really one:
they are today.

HARRIET BEECHER STOWE (BRAINYQUOTE,
N.D.)

I n the previous chapter, I shared with you how remaining
stuck in the past prevents us from creating and living the life
of our dreams. The past is an illusion because the only place
where it exists is within our minds and memories. Hence, we keep
the past alive by constantly mulling over it and reliving it in the
present.

Similarly, the future is also an illusion. Most people believe
that we cannot predict the future. I beg to differ; I can tell you
exactly what your future will be like. You will experience the
manifestation of your dominant thoughts, feelings, and emotions.
I'm not talking about the kind of thoughts, feelings, and emotions
you wish to have but the ones you are actually experiencing right
now. If you are constantly afraid your relationship with your
spouse will break down and you are constantly looking for

evidence of their infidelity, then a failed marriage awaits you in the future.

We experience strong emotions about future events by imagining those events playing out in the present moment. For instance, the suspicious spouse feels the dread and sinking feeling in their stomach as if the infidelity had already happened, even though their other half may be completely loyal to them. Hence, the future, just like the past, exists within our imagination. We can live and experience both only in the present moment, which corroborates the fact that the present moment is the only one that is real.

WHAT HAPPENS WHEN WE MANIFEST THE FUTURE?

When I was a newbie in the world of manifesting, I thought I was doing great by writing how everything I wanted would come to me. My manifestations hardly ever came to pass. I couldn't understand what the problem was. I was doing everything that the law of attraction books told me (or at least I thought I was).

It took me a while to understand that the issue was my use of future tense. I wasn't affirming, "I am grateful that I am thriving in my ideal career." Instead, I was saying, "I am grateful that I WILL thrive in my ideal career."

The problem with the use of future tense and espousing the idea that you will have something in the future is that you are supporting the idea that there is a lack of it right now. When you think about having something in the future, it is hard to feel absolute certainty. You can get yourself to believe there is a strong chance you will get what you want, but the feeling of absolute certainty is hard to evoke.

To feel certain that what you want will definitely be yours, you have to believe that what you want is already yours; it is not something that will come to you tomorrow, it is already yours in the here and now.

We always only manifest more of what we think and choose to feel. When you affirm a lack of something in the present moment, you manifest nothing but the lack. This eventually translates into you never getting what you desire.

YOU ARE THE ONLY ONE RESPONSIBLE FOR CREATING YOUR FUTURE

The Universe resides within you. Your imagination itself is the Universe. Hence, what you imagine is what you get. If you are to be brutally honest with yourself, you'll realize that every single thing in your life has sprung from your own imagination. The only problem was that you manifested many things you didn't want in the darkness of ignorance. It's okay because you really had no idea how powerful your imagination is.

You can shift and change your life dramatically right at this moment. You don't need money, power, or connections in the world to make things happen. The only connection that truly matters is the one you have with the Universe. The most powerful force in the entire Universe is your imagination. YOU have the power to turn the wheels of destiny in your favor and create the kind of life that you can only dream of.

The only prerequisite for becoming a master manifester is to use your imagination discerningly and to believe that what you want is already yours. If you can't get yourself to believe that what you want is already yours, then no one can help you. The laws of the Universe cannot be bent or changed. You have to live your life and go about your days as if whatever you had wished for has already come to pass. What does this look like? Let's discuss this in detail in the next section.

WHAT HAPPENS WHEN WE RECEIVE WHAT WE DESIRE?

Think about something you used to want very badly that is now yours. Maybe it is that designer handbag, that sports car, the dream house, or perhaps marrying your high school sweetheart. There was a time when you thought you would be the luckiest and happiest person in the world to have this one thing. Now, it is all yours. You feel gratitude and appreciation, but do you constantly and obsessively think about it?

Okay, I understand some people may say "yes" to this question, but I am also sure that if they still obsessively think about it, then it is not because of how happy and grateful they are. Those obsessive thoughts stem from their fears of losing what they have. They fear this dream will be broken and what has finally come to them will be lost.

They do suspect the loss of the object of their desire and affection; they are manifesting it. Any thought that occurs obsessively and evokes a strong emotional response in us is guaranteed to manifest on the screen of life at one point or another.

Hence, it is very important to practice self-awareness so you are always careful with what you manifest. Whenever you find yourself thinking fearful thoughts, replace them by thinking that you already have what you want. Be fully present in this moment and evoke the state of the wish fulfilled. If you can develop a habit of doing this, then nothing can prevent you from getting what you want and retaining it in your life once you have received it.

The important thing to recognize here is that once you have something, you don't think about it that often. You know it is already yours, so there is a sense of security around it. Whenever you think about it, you feel contentment and gratitude. This is the way you must live when you try to manifest something.

Obsessively thinking about the object of your desire and compulsively trying to manifest it in your future simply reinforces the idea that you do not have it. Lack creates more lack; there are no two ways about it. This is why dropping the desire by releasing all attachment to when and how it will come to pass is just as important as planting the seed by rooting yourself in the state of the wish fulfilled. I'm not suggesting that you have to force yourself to not think about what you want. Anything you try to force into existence is bound to fail. I am simply suggesting that you get yourself into the habit of asking yourself, "What would I think about right now, how would I live my life right now, what choices would I make in the present moment—if what I wanted was already mine?"

By getting yourself into the habit of thinking like this, you can counteract the obsession with trying to get something in the future. Besides, if you can't convince your mind through imagination that you already have what you desire, you will likely never get it. Every time you try to manifest something into the future, you simply push the goal post further away because you are manifesting not your desire but the idea that one day you'll have your desire.

That future will never come because there is no future. All that exists is this moment, the here and now. This is where all manifestations—all your dreams, desires, and aspirations—come from. It is up to you to reclaim them by fully embracing your power as the creator of your Universe. All you have to do is accept fully, completely, and wholly that all you want is already yours!

THE PAST AND THE FUTURE ARE THE EGO'S BEST FRIEND

The ego gives us a sense of identity in this material world. There is nothing wrong with having an ego. It's an essential aspect of the human experience. It's only through the ego that we get a chance to express our individuality in this world.

The problem is that the ego often picks up a lot of negative beliefs and limitations. It keeps us trapped in the past and compels us to think negatively about the future. The best way to trespass the trappings of the ego is to become fully present in the here and now. The breathing exercise I shared with you in the previous chapter is very helpful for this. Our breath is our connection with the Universe. By becoming conscious of our breathing by focusing all our attention on it, we also reinforce our connection with the Universe.

It's impossible to feel powerful when we obsess over the future or regret the past because change and transformation can occur only in the present moment. When you think about the past or the future, you are disconnected from your inner power. You think of things and events as happening to you instead of claiming your power as the creator of your Universe and all your life experiences. Feelings of guilt, hurt, pain, suffering, fear, and regret cloud your vision, and you find it hard to feel the eternal joy of the soul.

The soul is pure in its essence. All the experiences you identify as negative cannot do more than cloud the sun that shines eternally inside your heart. The soul is eternally pure; it is perfect in every way. By becoming fully present in this moment, you can feel the purity and perfection of your soul. From this pure soul, all things emerge.

To reclaim our power as the creator of your Universe, you must stop identifying with your ego. Whenever we identify with the ego, we identify with the past, with who we were and what happened to us, and it casts a shadow into the future. This further limits us from experiencing the manifestation of our desires. Don't forget that you can, be, have or do just about whatever you want. There are absolutely no limits in the Universe.

DO YOU ALWAYS HAVE TO BE FULLY PRESENT IN THE HERE AND NOW TO MANIFEST YOUR DESIRES?

Forcing your mind to do anything, be it obsessing over your manifestations or avoiding thinking about them, is a surefire way of making it rebel against you. Instead, everything must be done with gentle persuasion.

The first step of gentle persuasion is practicing heightened self-awareness. Instead of allowing yourself to become inundated by a deluge of random thoughts, check in every couple of hours or even several times within an hour on what you are thinking about. If you don't want a particular thought or fear to manifest, then simply train yourself to think and feel the opposite.

I know it can seem difficult at first, but as is the case with most things in life, you get better at it with time. On that note, I'm not suggesting that there will come a point where you won't get any negative thoughts about the past or the future. Such thoughts are part of the human experience in this dimension of reality. However, what will change is the frequency and intensity of those thoughts. They simply won't bother you as much, and you'll easily be able to switch gears.

I also don't want you to fear every negative thought you get. Just stand aside and observe your thoughts emerging and subsiding inside your mind like waves in the ocean. As long as you can inculcate and practice the witness mindset, they won't affect you. Interestingly, you'll start observing them subside just as quickly as they emerge. The only time they stick around for long is when you start obsessing about them. Hence, don't ask yourself why you are thinking about it or penalize yourself for having those thoughts. Just observe them like a bystander.

The two times of the day when I want you to be extra careful about what you think and feel are early in the morning right when you wake up and at night right before you fall asleep. At these two times of the day, the doorways of the subconscious remain wide open, and you are a lot likelier to experience your thoughts manifesting into a reality. Throughout the day, when the conscious mind is more in charge, not every thought or feeling that accompanies it has the power to manifest into physical reality. That being said, I'm not suggesting that you can afford to be callous with your mental, emotional, or psychological diet at any time of the day. You should be as mindfulness as you possibly can be at all hours of the day, but if you do end up falling from grace, it is better to let it happen during the day than in the early morning or late night hours when your subconscious is in charge and the seeds of manifestation can be sewn readily.

EXERCISE

Write down everything you want to manifest in the present tense. Remove words like "will," "may," "tomorrow," "someday," and "in the future." Instead, begin each sentence, "I am extremely grateful, happy, and excited that..."

After writing your manifestations, visualize and feel each word as if it is already true.

Create an imaginary act that reaffirms the idea that you already have what you desire. Replay it in your imagination every morning and night, fully evoking the state of the wish fulfilled.

Always think, feel, and act in the present moment. When you feel disconnected from the here and now, bring your focus to your breathing. Your breath will help ground your body, mind, and spirit to the present moment.

CHAPTER 5

TRYING TO MEDDLE WITH THE MIDDLE

> When you drop your desire in consciousness as a seed, confident that it shall appear in its full-blown potential, you have done all that is expected of you. To be worried or concerned about the manner of their unfoldment is to hold these fertile seeds in a mental grasp and, therefore, to prevent them from really maturing to full harvest.

NEVILLE GODDARD (YOUR FAITH IS YOUR FORTUNE, 2018)

The ego loves control. It makes us believe we need to twist and manipulate events if we want to get something. This is far from the truth. We have the power to attract whatever we desire. The keyword here is "attract." You cannot manifest your desires into your reality by applying force.

As I explained to you in detail in Chapter 1, for you to get what you want, there is only one requisite. You have to get yourself into the state of the wish fulfilled. You must use your imagination to live in the end—a point in time right after your desire has been fulfilled. Once you are there, you have to saturate that imaginal act of living in the end with all the overtones and undertones of reality. You must experience the scene from a first person perspective taking in all the details around you as if you were truly living inside that moment in time.

If you can successfully see yourself living in the state of the wish fulfilled, then there is absolutely no force in the Universe that can prevent you from getting what you want. The very first time you do the imaginal act, you have planted a seed. This seed will inevitably turn into a full-grown tree at the right time. However, you cannot dictate *how* your desires will come to pass, by what means, and exactly at which hour.

The Universe operates in its own timing. Your obsession with your manifestation will not hasten the process, but it can definitely delay it. As we discussed in the previous chapter, every time you find yourself obsessing over your manifestation, in truth, you are affirming the lack of it in your life. Lack begets lack; focusing on any idea or feeling of lack will take you further away from getting what you desire.

A BRIDGE OF INCIDENTS MUST UNFOLD

You cannot go from where you are to the reality you want to manifest in the blink of an eye. It is a process that involves several incidents that may seem disconnected at first, but in hindsight they all fit in together like pieces of a grand puzzle.

Once you have planted the seed by doing the imaginal act and saturating your subconscious by playing it on repeat, you should relax in the conviction that what you want is already yours. It is only a matter of time that your desire will manifest into your physical reality. In the meantime, every single incident that happens only takes you closer to your manifestation, even if it doesn't feel so right now. Things hardly ever make sense in the heat of the moment. Only when we look back do we realize how each moment is carefully built upon the other. If even one small incident happened differently, the course of our life may have been completely different.

Hence, your focus should be to remain strong in your conviction that what you want is already yours. Train yourself to live in the state of the wish fulfilled and to exercise radical faith even in the absence of any material evidence. I know ignoring the 3D reality can be very challenging, especially in those moments when it seems like your life is spiraling in the opposite direction of what you are trying to create. I always say that if you can't think positively about something, then just don't think about it. How do you do that? It's quite simple: keep yourself very busy!

The most important thing is to keep yourself in a high vibrational state of positivity, happiness, love, and hope. When you are excited about life, you are in a high vibrational state. When you feel positive, happy, and hopeful, you are in a high vibrational state. When your heart is filled with love, compassion, and gratitude, you are in a high vibrational state.

Your desires are magnetically attracted to you when you vibrate at a higher frequency. On the contrary, depressed and unhappy people attract negative situations, things, and people into their lives. In every moment, you have the power to choose who you want to be and what you want to attract. You must wield your power with awareness. Don't allow any negative thought to bog you down; replace it quickly with a positive one.

If it seems hard to stay in a positive mental and emotional state, then do something that makes you happy. The world outside is only a reflection of the world inside. There is no need to fear any random thing happening in your life. You are fully in charge of your destiny and your future. The Universe must abide by your will, but you must practice your will by choosing your thoughts, feelings, and emotions carefully—not just once in a while but every single moment of every day!

EXERCISES FOR TRANSFORMING NEGATIVE THOUGHTS AND EMOTIONS

You can use just one or two of the methods below, or both of them. Pick the one that works best for you or simply try out both.

Method 1:

Write down the negative thoughts that bother you, allowing yourself to feel them as deeply as possible. Allow all negative emotions that follow to come to the surface.

Think about the exact opposite (which you actually want to experience) and write them down as affirmations. Make sure that all affirmations are written in the present tense. For instance, if your negative thought is "I will fail the driving test." Your new positive affirmation can be: "I am so grateful and happy that I have passed my driving test so easily and effortlessly."

Do this exercise for every negative thought. Whenever the thoughts start plaguing you again, read the positive affirmations you have created to counteract them. You must read with feeling, allowing each word to evoke an emotional response and vivid mental imagery in you. In other words, while reading, you must train yourself to feel as if the words were already true.

Method 2:

If you are struggling with overwhelmingly negative thoughts that seem to occur randomly and in an unrelated fashion, then you can try a technique to manifest a positive state of mind.

Create a scene where someone else is affirming to you how positive you are. For instance, you could be having a conversation with your mother. In the imaginal act, she says to you, "Isn't it truly wonderful, Jane, how positive and happy you always are. I am amazed by how quickly your desires manifest into physical reality."

In your mind, you'll keep replaying this scene over and over again until it begins to feel real. If you can plant this seed of positivity through this imaginal act, then your mental and emotional state will change!

EXERCISE: MAINTAINING A HIGH VIBRATIONAL STATE

Take a sheet of paper and write down everything you wish you had done or want to do, every desire that you've had to try something out. Don't think about how viable or practical it is to do it now. If it has ever crossed your mind, then it is good enough to be on your list. This can be anything from piano lessons to paragliding or even wildlife photography.

Keep this list with you at all times. You can keep adding to it whenever new ideas crop up in your mind. You can also slash off anything that you have really lost interest in.

Whenever you find yourself obsessing over your manifestation or you feeling negative, frustrated, or depressed, pick one item from this list and try it out. It can be something big or small, depending upon what you feel like doing. If the task is huge, like learning how to play a piano, just take the first step right now. For instance, you can research and contact teachers online.

The point of this exercise is to focus and direct your energy into constructive channels of creativity. Whenever you do things you like and enjoy, you automatically shift into a high vibrational state. Retaining a high vibrational state is as simple as staying joyful the majority of the time, if not always (but then, we are human!). It is okay to fall down at times, but you must make yourself resilient enough to immediately get up, brush your knees, and get back to business. You can do it; I believe in you!

POSITIVE AND NEGATIVE EVENTS ARE ESSENTIAL COMPONENTS OF THE BRIDGE OF INCIDENTS

Most people do the imaginal act, and the moment it seems as if something is happening in their reality that doesn't fit in with what they are trying to manifest, they abandon their faith and conviction. To become highly skilled at manifesting, you must never do this!

The ways of the Universe are much greater than our ways and our limited understanding. We think that things have to unfold in a particular sequence for us to get the thing we desire, but the Universe always knows better. Often, the shortest, most effective, and perfect route to our manifestation is one that is totally beyond our imagination. You have to trust that once you have planted the seed by doing the imaginal act, your job is done. Now, it is up to the Universe to figure out how to bridge the gap between you and your manifestation. If there is just one thing you take away from this chapter, let it be this: the Universe always chooses the shortest and best route to get you to your manifestation!

I know all too well how hard it can be to believe this when it seems like things are falling apart faster than you can wrap your head around them. But trust me, every time you plant a seed of manifestation and it seems like everything in your world has started falling apart, it is simply the Universe rearranging the fabric of your personal Universe for you. Things will come back together, and they will be better than ever! In the end, everything ALWAYS works out. You just have to retain your faith and keep moving on the path of manifestation.

One of my most favorite quotes is a verse from the Hebrew Bible: "Now faith is the substance of things hoped for, the evidence of things not seen" (Hebrews 11:1 - King James Version, n.d.). It doesn't matter whether you are religious or not; this isn't about faith in something outside of yourself. The entire Universe is present within you. This is about trusting the power of the Universe that lives and breathes within you in the form of your magnificent human imagination. Through the power of the imagination, you can create anything you desire.

Because of the gross nature of this "reality," things may take a little time to manifest, but they will surely come to pass. After successfully imagining the state of the wish fulfilled, the Universe will guide you to take inspired action wherever it is needed. For that, you must avoid all desire to manipulate your immediate reality to coax the Universe into giving you what you desire.

For instance, let's say that you have had a fallout with your best friend. He has blocked your number, and there is no way for you to contact him. You create a scene for the state of the wish fulfilled: you and your best friend are happily enjoying a beach vacation in Hawaii. Even though there is no evidence in your current reality that this scene will come to pass, you hold on to it by replaying it in your imagination. A few days later, you get a strong feeling; it's as if the Universe is prompting you to do something. It doesn't make any sense, but you feel a strong urge to go outside for a walk in the park. In the park, you see your friend. You walk up to him and apologize for the misunderstanding that happened. You make up, and your friend asks you if you'd join him for a vacation in Hawaii. Before you realize it, the end that you had imagined has become your reality.

The important thing to note here is that everything happened seamlessly. You did the imaginal act and then got busy living your life. When you got the urge to go for a walk in the park, you had no idea why you were doing it. You just felt inspired to do it. Even when it came to delivering an apology, you felt an intuitive urge to do it. There was a strong conviction in your heart that it was the right thing to do.

Now, imagine the opposite. You did the imaginal act, and soon after, you started hunting for evidence that it was working. You waited patiently for a few days, and when it seemed like nothing was happening, you decided it would be a good idea to drop by your friend's house. You go over and the moment they see you at the door, they are furious with rage. You try your best to deliver an apology, but they won't have a single word from you. You are left thinking this isn't how it should have turned out. After all, you did the imaginal act! Things should have healed by now.

In this case, you are deliberately trying to manipulate events to suit your objective. The Universe will never support you in this. Hence, what you are actually doing is creating a blockage that prevents the manifestation from occurring. Either your manifestation will be delayed, or it simply won't happen. You must relinquish control by allowing the Universe to work for you. Your job is only to imagine and believe that what you want has been given to you. If any action must be taken, then it has to be intuitively inspired and not deliberately selected.

Every incident will eventually fit into the big picture to take you to your manifestation. You must keep your sight fixed on what you desire and ignore all evidence of its lack in your current 3D reality. I'm not saying that you have to live in the state of the wish fulfilled at all times. All I am saying is that you must remain fully present in the here and now for the vast majority of the day. Again, the breathing exercise I taught you in the previous chapter is extremely useful. Devote your time and energy to self-improvement. This way, you simply won't have enough time to be obsessed with what is happening or not happening with your manifestation.

Whenever your mind starts telling you that what you want will never happen, ask yourself a simple question: "Is there any clear evidence that what I want will never happen?" You obviously don't have any evidence, right? Then ask yourself: "Is there any clear evidence that what I want will definitely happen?"

Again, the answer is no! When both the ideas require an investment of faith in your part, which is a better idea to believe in? If you don't have evidence that you will get what you want and you don't have evidence that you won't get what you want, isn't it better to believe in the former?

EXERCISE

Start paying attention to your intuition. Observe what it tells you and what it prompts you to do. You don't have to classify yourself as an intuitive person in order to have a strong intuition. Every single one of us has been endowed with an equally powerful intuition. The more you pay attention to the prompts of your intuition, the sharper it becomes.

CHAPTER 6
HOLDING ONTO A NEGATIVE SELF-IMAGE

" What lies behind us and what lies before us are but tiny matters compared to what lies within us.

RALPH WALDO EMERSON (PASSITON.COM, N.D.)

The world outside is a perfect reflection of the world within. Trying to change things in the outer world without attempting any change within is like fighting with your reflection in the mirror instead of making changes to your appearance. No matter how hard you fight the circumstances in your external world, nothing will change until you change the ideas and beliefs that give birth to them. Transforming your life is an inside out project.

The most important factor that influences your reality is the self-image you carry within. Your self-image is the sum total of all those core beliefs and ideas you have about yourself. Everything you believe you are, can do, and cannot do combine together to work as your self-image.

YOU CAN'T CHANGE ANYTHING LONG-TERM WITHOUT TRANSFORMING YOUR SELF-IMAGE

If you want financial security but your self-image dictates that you identify as a poor person, then you can never experience an over-abundance of money. Even if you manage to manifest money into your reality, you won't be able to hold onto it for long. This is because your reality must always be a perfect match to your self-image.

Another example would be a salesman who believes he can easily earn a commission of $100,000 in a year but believes it is impossible for a person of his stature to make $200,000 in commissions. This salesman may have a few weeks that are exceptional. He makes so much money that if the sales remain consistent, he can easily cross the $200,000 mark in that year. But since his self-image is aligned with another belief, once he hits the $100,000 mark, or gets close to it, sales slow down or simply stop happening.

No matter what you are experiencing right now, it is a perfect match to the self-image you have formed. You may not be consciously aware of this self-image, but it is nevertheless present inside you. If you want to know what your future will be like, then you have to analyze the current self-image you have. No matter how many affirmations you do for the results you want to create in your life, nothing will work long-term if you don't first transform your self-image.

You can't manifest a great marriage if you have the self-image of a lonely heartbroken person whom every lover eventually abandons. No matter how many new romantic interests you manage to attract into your life, you will experience the same story with every person because they are only the actors in the movie of your life. It is you who is the writer and director of your life's script.

There's a reason why a multi-millionaire loses all his money and then makes it all back in a matter of six months. The multi-millionaire retains the self-image of a wealthy person even when he is broke. Hence, his reality must eventually match the self-image he carries within. He sees making money as a game, something that can be easily done and is a fun activity to indulge in. Hence, money flows to him abundantly and easily.

On the other hand, another person may struggle to make even a $1 a day because they consider themselves poor and miserable. Their self-image dictates the idea that money is something that others have. They view money as something that's very hard to make.

A poor self-image is also the reason why people who win large amounts of money in a lottery manage to blow it all off in no time and go back to being the poor person they were before.

What you have and the situations you experience exist because of who you perceive yourself to be. If you want your life to change, then you have to start by changing your self-perception. The biggest mistake that both beginners and advanced practitioners of the law of attraction make is that they focus entirely on the results they want to manifest without altering the self-image that has been preventing them from getting what they want.

EXERCISE

Create a list of the things you are struggling to manifest.

Analyze each item on the list, and write down all the self-image ideas and beliefs that are tied to that manifestation. For instance, if you want to manifest a new job, does your self-image say you are jobless and unemployable?

You have to be honest with yourself to do this exercise properly. It is often hard to identify and accept how we contribute to our own miseries. In fact, we are the only ones who create our reality. You must assume responsibility and take ownership for everything you have manifested in your life. This is the only way you will manifest the life of your dreams. It all begins with believing that the power to create anything and everything lies within you!

Start becoming observant of your inner dialogue. How do you talk to yourself? Is that talk uplifting and empowering or does it bog you down?

Also listen to how you talk about yourself to others. Do you often portray yourself as a victim to be pitied or do you come across as a strong, confident person?

By becoming aware of your current self-image, you can begin the process of transforming it. By accepting and embracing where you currently are, you jumpstart the process of transforming the self-image that has given birth to the undesirable circumstances you are going through right now.

HOW TO CREATE YOUR DESIRED SELF-IMAGE

Since you have picked this book, I assume you already know a fair bit about the law of attraction. Hence, you must already be familiar with the importance of having a vision board representing your ideal lifestyle. In case you don't know what I am talking about, I will explain what a vision board is.

A vision board is a collection of images you put together to represent your ideal life. It can be either digital or an actual physical board. I strongly recommend having a physical vision board, as there is something powerful about having a tactile representation of your ideal life. You should hang your vision board on a wall that you face for the maximum amount of hours in your day, such as opposite your work desk.

In other words, you want to get yourself so used to looking at those images that they begin to seep deep into your subconscious. Thereby, eventually, they will influence and dictate your reality.

Where most people go wrong is that they focus entirely on the images of the results they are trying to get. They forget to include pictures that represent their ideal self-image. The exercise that I will share now is extremely powerful for building your self-image from the ground up. Don't take it lightly. This exercise can quite literally change your life and skyrocket your manifestation success. Whatever you want to have will come to you when you have a self-image that matches it.

EXERCISE

Pick at least three people who possess the characteristics you wish to emulate and/or who are living the kind of life you want to live. Start studying their lives; try to learn as much as you can by reading books and watching videos about them. If your list includes someone you know in real life, simply start observing how they act, move, behave, and respond to different circumstances.

Collect pictures of these people that represent to you the characteristics that you want to have in yourself. For instance, if you are inspired by Muhammad Ali's exercise regime, then you can add an image of Ali exercising in the gym to your vision board. They don't have to quite literally be doing specific activities, but the image must remind you of the characteristics that inspire you.

Spend ten minutes every morning (right after waking up) and evening (before going to bed, after completing your evening routine) visualizing yourself doing similar things that confirm to your mind that you now possess those characteristics that you admire in these people.

Do this exercise consistently for at least 180 days. It is really a fun exercise to do that will make you feel good. I strongly recommend that you continue this exercise for the rest of your life. Of course, you can change/add/remove people that inspire you and the characteristics you are trying to incorporate in yourself. But if you do this only for a limited period of time, then do it every single day for the next 180 days.

I can guarantee you won't be the same person at the end of the 180-day period, nor will your life remain the same. You will be amazed by how far you have come and by who you become. It's an investment of twenty minutes every day to do something truly enjoyable and inspiring that has the power to completely change your life!

USING AFFIRMATIONS TO FURTHER REINFORCE YOUR NEW SELF-IMAGE

Affirmations—positive statements that you repeat often—are a powerful tool for transforming the subconscious mind. You likely already use affirmations to manifest the things you desire. I suggest you take things up a notch and start using it to also manifest the person you want to be. After all, you'll have to be a person with certain specific characteristics in order to have and enjoy the things you desire.

As I shared in the previous chapter, affirmations have to always be written in the present tense. So it'll never be, "I will become..." You will always say "I am..."

 I AM two of the most powerful words, for what you put after them shapes your reality.

BEVAN LEE (THE MINDS JOURNAL, N.D.)

I think this quote perfectly summarizes the power contained within the words "I am." Be careful when you say these two words, whether out aloud or inside your mind. You are not just making a statement; you are dictating your reality and defining the situations/experiences/people that will be attracted to you. What we experience is never separated from who we are. Hence, we must be careful with the words we choose to place after these two most important words.

EXERCISE

Write down affirmations for the characteristics you wish to incorporate in yourself. If you have completed the previous exercise, you will know what those characteristics are. Make sure you write the affirmations in the present tense as if what you are saying is already true for you.

For instance, if you wish to be more self-disciplined and goal-oriented, then your affirmation can be: I am extremely disciplined, focused, motivated, and goal-oriented.

If you want to become an early riser, then your affirmation can be: I love waking up at 4 a.m. (or whatever time you would like to start waking up at) and getting to the grind early.

TRANSFORMING NEGATIVE SELF-IMAGE THROUGH AFFIRMATIONS

You can use affirmations not just to build your desired self-image but also to transform your existing negative self-image into a positive one. Becoming conscious of your inner dialogue is the most important step toward transforming your self-image. You are who you think and believe you are. If you can convince yourself that you are a different person than who you have been telling yourself you are, then nothing can prevent your reality from undergoing a massive 180-degree shift.

EXERCISE

Every time you find yourself putting negative words after the "I am," pause for a moment and observe what is happening. Write down those words and then write the exact opposite of it on a fresh sheet of paper. For instance, let's say your mind is saying "I am so stupid." You can write the opposite that you would like to have as the truth: "I am extremely smart and intelligent."

Once you have written down the new positive affirmations, burn the original sheet that had the negative self-affirmations. Yes, you can do this exercise digitally as well, but there is really something powerful about doing this exercise on a physical sheet of paper and releasing your old self by burning the sheet and immersing the ashes in running water (like a river or even your bathroom flush maybe). You can also just throw the ashes in the garden, where they will become one with the soil. This ritual signifies the demise of your old self, and the new affirmations celebrate your rebirth as the type of person you want to be.

LOVE YOURSELF UNCONDITIONALLY

A lot of people think self-improvement is something akin to self-sabotage. They assume that any desire to be better comes from self-loathing. Since this entire chapter has been about the importance of self-image and how you can cultivate your ideal self-image, I feel it is important to include a note on how critical it is to love yourself unconditionally.

Indeed, I've asked you to become more attentive to what kind of statements you say about yourself and the current self-image that is preventing you from receiving your manifestations in "real" life. But I must warn you against becoming judgmental of yourself. Who you are right now and the self-image you have developed so far is a result of all your life experiences. From a young age, you were conditioned to be a specific kind of person by people who didn't know any better themselves. You have to forgive yourself for having this negative self-image. You didn't know any better until now.

Becoming observant doesn't imply feeling guilty or blaming yourself. It simply means witnessing the ebb and flow of thoughts as if they are waves in an ocean. Let them arise and let them go. Problems begin the moment we start trying to micro-analyze each thought. Why am I getting this thought? How can I think like this? What's wrong with me?

The desire to become a better version of yourself should never come from a place of self-loathing. In that case, true happiness will remain forever elusive to you. You'll find tremendous joy and happiness in your self-improvement efforts when the desire to be better than who you were yesterday comes from a place of deep self-love. Take inspiration from others and seek to incorporate into your own self the qualities you admire most about them. BUT, don't compare yourself with anyone. Your only competition should be with the person you were yesterday.

Accept and love yourself unconditionally. Something really magical happens when you begin to truly practice this. Your world is a reflection of yourself. How you treat yourself is how others will treat you. When you begin to truly accept and love yourself unconditionally, other people will also accept and love you unconditionally.

EXERCISE

Take a sheet of paper and write down the following affirmation twenty-one times every day for the next three days:

I accept myself unconditionally. I love myself unconditionally.

To make it even more powerful, you can repeat it twenty-one times every morning (right after waking up) while looking into your eyes in the mirror. This is an extremely powerful exercise. I strongly recommend you continue this practice for at least the next twenty-one days and possibly for the rest of your life!

Also, whenever you find yourself engaged in a negative dialogue with yourself, remind yourself of this affirmation and start saying it to yourself (out aloud or quietly inside your mind).

CHAPTER 7
IMAGINING FROM THE THIRD PERSON PERSPECTIVE

 To bring anything into your life, imagine that it's already there.

RICHARD BACH (BRAINYQUOTE, N.D.)

Visualization combined with faith that you already have what you desire is the most important tool for manifestation. It is a common practice amongst law of attraction practitioners to visualize their desire in the form of a movie. They see themselves getting what they desire inside their mind's eye in a way that feels akin to watching a movie.

I am strongly against this method.

If you are using any method of visualization that involves seeing yourself getting what you desire from a third person perspective, there is a 50 percent chance you won't get it. I am saying 50 percent and not 100 percent because it is still possible you will receive your manifestation due to other factors (like if you have a strong assumption about it). The problem with this method is that it disjoints you from the scene you are visualizing.

In "real" life you don't look at yourself getting or experiencing something. You are inside the scene living within your body. To see yourself as another person getting what you desire can impress the idea upon your subconscious that you want to see someone else receive the manifestation. I have experienced this myself, and many of my family, friends, colleagues, and acquaintances will testify this: when you see yourself receiving your manifestation as a third person watching yourself, it is highly likely that's exactly how the scene will play out in real life. In other words, you will bear witness to someone receiving the manifestation you are trying to create for yourself, but it may or may not be you.

WHAT NOT TO DO

As I said earlier, even when you visualize yourself as a person receiving the manifestation, there is a 50 percent chance that you will get it. This is because visualization is only one aspect of the manifestation process (albeit the most important one). Other factors, like the strength of your assumption and your faith that you have already received what you desire, can help you receive the manifestation, even if you don't follow the visualization process exactly.

However, if you are reading this book, chances are you struggle with manifesting your desires. One by one, we are troubleshooting your methods and processes to diagnose all the proverbial chinks in your armor. Alongside the troubleshooting, I am also teaching you the most reliable and time-tested methods of manifestation that work every single time.

If you do the manifestation properly (as it is laid out in Chapter 1), then you will get the results. There are no exceptions to this rule. Manifestation, when done properly, is a highly scientific method that produces the desired results every single time. In this chapter, I will help you further refine your visualization techniques so that you get the desired results 100 percent of the time.

To foolproof your visualization technique, you have to avoid resorting to any method that involves seeing yourself from a third person perspective because, as I've said, what you are really manifesting is being a third party witness to someone else receiving the manifestation.

PREPARING FOR THE VISUALIZATION

The first step you must take toward successful visualization is defining with as much clarity as possible exactly what you want to achieve. It should ideally be a scene that takes place after your desire has been fulfilled. Another important thing to consider while outlining the scene is that it should be something that can be played on a loop.

For instance, if you desire to be extremely wealthy, living a life of freedom, while traveling the world on your private jet, then you can create a scene where you are sitting inside your private jet. You look out the window and the city of London (or whichever) below you as the jet takes off. A little while later, the flight attendant appears before you with a drink. You take the drink from her, and she says to you with a smile on her face, "Welcome on board Mr./Miss (your name)."

Let's take another instance into consideration. Let's say you want to heal a knee injury (yes, you can heal some diseases and physical pain through manifestation), and there is nothing you would like to do more than get back on the basketball court. You can visualize yourself enjoying playing basketball. You think to yourself that this feels so amazing, and you throw the ball into the basket, feeling a sense of victory.

There are two key aspects to both of these scenes:

1. They both occur at a point after the manifested desire has materialized. You are on a private jet because you have already created a life of financial freedom and abundance. You are playing basketball because your

knee is perfectly healthy. Yes, a lot of people visualize the scene of the desire getting fulfilled, but I find this to be a far more effective method that gets results 100 percent of the time. Think of an event that can occur only after your desire has been fulfilled and craft a scene around it.

2. These scenes both are laid out in such a way that you can play them on an endless loop. Your scene shouldn't be any more than 3-5 seconds long. It should be easy to remember. For instance, you can keep hearing the "Welcome on board Mr./Miss (your name)" over and over again. You can keep throwing the ball through the basket over and over again.

If you can create a scene that meets both of these criteria, then you are starting out on solid ground. If you can visualize the scene in a loop as you fall asleep at night, then there is absolutely no force in the world that can prevent you from getting your desire.

THINK OF WHAT YOU ACTUALLY WANT

I will now share with you some more important tips, tricks, ideas, and techniques to further strengthen your visualization technique.

You want to create the scene around what you actually want and not around titles or positions you think you want. For instance, one of my friends came to me saying that she wanted to become the CEO of her company. When we delved deeper into it, she realized that what she truly wanted was to be in an influential position. She wanted to make a lot of money, travel the world, and have a say in how the company was operating.

Now, what do you think she really wanted? Was it the title of CEO, financial freedom, the ability to travel the world, being able to make the impact, etc.? Obviously, she wanted the latter. Hence, when you are manifesting, you must think of the traits that are part of the manifestation you desire.

Write down exactly the kind of experiences you want to have using the characteristics of the thing you desire. What do you expect to get out of the thing you desire? Whatever thoughts and emotions come up at that time, that's what you want to write down.

You have to ask yourself how you want to feel when your desire becomes your reality. Making this distinction between what we want and how we actually want to feel and experience is important. A lot of times, I thought I wanted a specific thing, but once I got it, I hated it. I realized it wasn't the thing that I wanted but the feeling I thought I would have when I got it. It's not necessary that you desire a specific title, job, degree or whatever. It is best to focus on the end goal once you're there—what you want to feel, think, and experience if what you desire were already yours.

Once you have nailed down the final experience you desire, you can create a scene that represents the state of the wish fulfilled. Again, it is absolutely crucial that you don't construct a scene outlining a middle. For instance, the title of the CEO is actually a middle. The end result my friend desired was financial freedom, work satisfaction, and the ability to travel the world. When we imagine the end, the Universe will figure out how to fill the middle in the most perfect manner possible. In fact, it often happens in a way that we didn't imagine or expect.

In my friend's case, we constructed a scene where she was skiing in a luxurious resort in Switzerland with her ten-year-old son by her side. In the visualization, she thinks about how amazing her life is and then hits the ski slope (in the present tense). She played the scene of hitting the ski slope in a loop over and over again. The scene implied that she already had all the things she desired—financial freedom, etc.

Interestingly enough, a few months later, things just fell into place in the most incredible manner. She didn't become the CEO of the company she was working with; instead, she ended up partnering with an ex-college mate. The money and the work satisfaction came on their own eventually.

This is why it is very important to focus on what you want to experience and feel rather than trying to dictate the source from which it should all come.

EXERCISE: TECHNIQUES FOR GETTING INTO FIRST PERSON PERSPECTIVE

Whatever we impress upon the subconscious, the exact likeness of it will be produced in physical reality. It is like using a photo-copying machine. The real you is not this; it is the awareness inside of you that is far bigger than the ego self or the name that you identify with. This awareness is the Universe itself. It is this awareness that manifests everything.

Hence, you must manifest from the perspective of the awareness that resides within you. In other words, you have to visualize the state of the wish fulfilled, from the point of view of the person who receives the manifestation. You must look through your own eyes and not at yourself.

When you are ready to do the visualization, you want to step away entirely from this current reality. So no thinking, "Oh no! I have to wake up early," "I can't do this right now," "I have so much on my plate," and so on. Focus your awareness entirely on the present moment, not on what you have to get done. The best way to concentrate your focus in the present moment is by focusing entirely on your breath.

Use the breathing exercise I outlined in Chapter 3 by counting to four with each inhale and exhale. As you begin focusing on your breath, get yourself in a comfortable position. You could be sitting down or lying down—either is fine. Just make sure that you don't fall asleep. The idea is to enter a state of deep relaxation while remaining aware of your surroundings and of yourself.

Allow yourself to relax completely by taking full breaths.

Continue counting with each inhale and exhale. Don't hurry through this; you will have remnants of this present reality left with you. For instance, your mind will still remain semi-fixated on the things you want to do today, tomorrow, or next week. Can you still manifest with all these things going on? Yes, but we are talking about the most effective and foolproof technique that is guaranteed to get you results every single time.

Once you become fully relaxed, you are ready to start the visualization. The first step is to get inside your body in the first person perspective. With your eyes closed, imagine your palms in front of your face, the exact way you would look at them right now if your eyes were open. You won't be seeing yourself looking at your hands; you'll be inside your body looking at your hands through your own eyes.

Now, look down at your feet, using your mind's eye. Observe your chest, stomach, and groin. Scan your body up and down while you are inside it looking at yourself from your own eyes. If you want to make this exercise even more effective, then you can add some animation to it by doing something actively while inside your body. For instance, you can tighten your belt, tie your shoelace, slip your feet into your shoes, smooth the wrinkles on your skirt, etc. The point of this exercise is to not just experience the scene from the first person perspective but also to become quite literally lost inside it. You want to immerse yourself in this reality to such an extent that the present reality fades away completely.

Oftentimes, the visuals are either dark or unclear. This is not an issue. The important thing is to *know* that you are doing it; if you know it, then that means you are doing the visualization right. It is the feeling that matters most. However, in the best case scenario, you'd be able to see the visuals clearly. You can gradually train your imagination to be able to do so. If your mind wanders, don't judge it or be too hard on yourself. Gently bring it back to the present moment every time.

Now that you have fully stepped into first person perspective, it is time to start doing the actual visualization. Make sure you have the scene written down. It will help you visualize with a greater degree of clarity when you are inside the scene. I have struggled with visualizations myself when I fail to write them down.

Once you are inside this imaginal reality, it is time to play the scene in a loop. Whatever it is—kissing someone, shaking hands with someone, saying I love you—keep playing it over and over again until your mind becomes fully saturated with that reality.

As you become immersed into this new reality, add sensory vividness to the scene. Observe how the wall in front of you looks and feels, notice how your clothes feel against your skin, etc. Sensory vividness comes from filling in details about what you would experience if you stepped inside the scene with all your five senses in a heightened state of awareness, as it would feel if you were really present there.

You don't have to force yourself to feel anything in particular. If you do this properly by fully immersing yourself into that reality from a first person perspective, then the emotions will arise of their own accord. It would be exactly the way things happen in real life.

There will come a point when you feel satisfied and content. You don't have to feel any intense emotion. You are imagining a scene that is taking place after the desire has been fulfilled. The shock of getting what you want has already worn off. However, if you do not feel a sense of satisfaction and contentment, then that's also not an issue. Your manifestation is still guaranteed to come to pass, but if you feel a sense of satisfaction and contentment, then you can be doubly sure that you have successfully planted the seed.

CHAPTER 8
HOPING INSTEAD OF EXPECTING

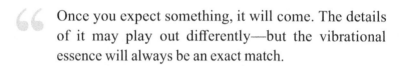 Once you expect something, it will come. The details of it may play out differently—but the vibrational essence will always be an exact match.

ESTHER & JERRY HICKS (ASK AND IT IS GIVEN: LEARNING TO MANIFEST YOUR DESIRES, 2004)

There is a massive difference between hoping and expecting. You hope to receive something when you are 50 percent sure you'll receive it and 50 percent unsure about it at the same time. Sometimes you think it will happen, other times you doubt it will ever come to pass. Expecting to receive your manifestation is a different story altogether. You start doing things in your immediate reality as if what you want was already yours.

There may be a delay from the time you do the visualization until the time you receive the manifestation, just like how there may be a delay in placing an order online and the moment it gets delivered to your doorstep. But once the order has been placed, you relax and let go. You know the order will arrive once it's ready. To successfully manifest your desires, you must practice the same level of conviction. To receive your manifestation, you must exercise faith.

HOW MANIFESTATIONS GET DELAYED (AND PERHAPS EVEN DENIED)

Not thinking at all about your manifestation is much better than thinking negatively about it. More often than not, our manifestations don't come to pass because we are standing in our own way. Be honest about it: Have you been having these kinds of thoughts? "I don't think that will happen." "How in the world will it ever come about?" "I just don't think it is in my destiny."

The problem with doubtful and negative thoughts is that they project negative energy onto the thing we are trying to manifest. Constantly worrying and thinking negatively also impacts our vibrational frequency. When we vibrate at a lower frequency, we are unable to attract something that is at a higher vibrational frequency simply because our frequencies don't match. In that case, no amount of effort at the physical level in the material world can attract that thing to us.

I am sure you have heard the saying "everything is energy." This statement is true. We are energy, and everything around us is energy. If you want anything in the material world, you must first attract it into your aura at an energetic level. If you can hold, acquire, and possess something in the energetic world, then there is absolutely no force in the world that can prevent it from showing up in your life at the material level.

The one thing you must try and avoid at all costs is negative thinking. I'm not saying that one single negative thought can kill your manifestation. It's just that obsessively thinking negatively about the possibility of receiving your manifestation will definitely delay it. I am sure you have noticed by now that it is always easier to receive the manifestations in which you aren't too invested. They usually come to pass far quicker than you would have thought possible. Even things that seemed too wild and impossible come to pass fairly quickly when you drop the desire and just get on with your life.

The best way to avoid negative thinking is simply by staying busy. Whenever negative thoughts begin to crop up, pick something from your wish list of things you want to do and just do it! I am referring to the exercise you completed in Chapter 5. If you haven't done it, then go back to that chapter and complete the exercise.

Another great way of maintaining a high vibrational frequency and shifting your focus away from the negative thoughts is by doing something for someone else. Find someone who needs your help and do something for them without expecting anything in return. Not only will you grow your good karma bank, but you'll also feel good about yourself. I'm not talking about feeling good about yourself in a self-applauding way but rather the sense of contentment that comes with knowing your life is meaningful and purposeful.

Besides, every good deed is rewarded handsomely by the Universe. Whenever we do something good for someone else without any personal agenda, the good comes back to us multiplied. You will not get that good karma if you do good deeds while expecting to receive anything back, however. The contentment, happiness, and satisfaction you receive from the act itself should be its own reward for you.

Hence, if you are struggling with doubts and fears regarding your manifestation, then it is better to not think at all about it than to think negatively about it. Engage your mind in productive tasks and try to stay content, happy, and joyful as much as possible throughout the day.

Surrendering to the Universe is essential. You can't control how your wish will come to fruition, very much like how you can't go into a restaurant's kitchen and dictate how your meal should be prepared. You specify to the waiter what you want, and you trust that the chef will prepare the dish you desire. The waiter eventually brings you the final product. It works the same way with the Universe. You have to allow the Universe to work on your behalf.

The key here is to trust the process and not overthink things. The manner in which the Universe will bring our desires to fruition is usually beyond our ability to comprehend. We can't dictate the timing for when our order will be delivered. All we can do is trust that our manifestation is already ours. When the time is right, we will see it and experience it in physical reality.

GETTING OUT OF THE SCARCITY MINDSET

We have been conditioned by family, teachers, and society that there are only a limited number of great things available in this world. From childhood, this idea is ingrained in our minds that we have to struggle hard to get anything valuable in life. We are told to dream "realistically" and to keep our feet on the ground.

This kind of thinking is the primary reason why we find it hard to truly believe that we can get what we desire. We hope we do, but we don't live our life as if we are truly expecting to receive it.

The journey from hoping to expecting is often not an easy one because it involves overriding or dismantling many of our limiting beliefs. These limiting beliefs often reside within the deepest trenches of our subconscious mind. They influence our life in ways we often don't understand. For instance, we may experience a strong dislike for something. We think it is because of the object or the person that we experience the dislike, but in reality, it is simply due to the programming that our subconscious mind has undergone.

Maybe, when you were growing up, you had a parent who disliked the thing you now desire and at the subconscious level, you adopted their dislike. It now feels like your own dislike or fear, but it actually came from your parent.

You have to start becoming conscious of this scarcity mindset. We all have it to some degree or another. Even if you don't have it in certain areas of life, you surely have it in other areas. For instance, I have come across a lot of women who believe that good men are impossible to find in today's world. Maybe you think the same and you are ready to argue that this really is the truth.

The belief that there aren't that many good men in this world is an idea like everything else in life. This idea defines and dictates your experiences with men. You automatically attract to yourself men who are not good because your subconscious mind is always on the lookout for those experiences that will validate your beliefs.

A woman who believes that there are many wonderful men in this world tends to meet and attract a lot of good men into her life. Her subconscious mind validates her beliefs by bringing her experiences that are aligned with the ideas she holds in her mind.

If there is any particular area of life where you are struggling to succeed, then you really need to sit back and analyze the beliefs you have surrounding that area of life. For instance, do you believe succeeding at business is hard? You are doing the visualizations and you are giving your absolute best to your work, but nothing seems to work out. Perhaps it is time to delve deeper into your beliefs about your business.

Your mind can create any reality you desire. It is the most powerful tool in the Universe. You must reclaim your power as the creator of your Universe by reclaiming your mind. If things aren't working out in any area of your life, then go deeper into understanding the beliefs that you hold for that area of life. Once you have identified those beliefs, work on transforming them by planting new positive beliefs in their place.

EXERCISE

Identify and write down all your beliefs and ideas that come from the scarcity mindset. If you aren't sure how to identify them, simply start paying attention to the chatter inside your mind when it tells you that you can't have, be, or do something you want. These could also be beliefs about other people. For instance, you may believe that good people are rare these days, most people are really selfish, or the rich get rich at the expense of the poor. I am sure you can identify many such ideas and beliefs once you start paying attention to your own mind.

Once you have written everything down, take a fresh sheet of paper and start writing the exact opposite of what you have written. For instance, if your old belief was "good people are rare to find these days," your new belief can be "there are so many good people in the world; I am constantly attracting the most wonderful people into my life." Similarly, for the belief "most people are really selfish," you can write "I always attract the most selfless, kind, and generous people into my life."

Do this exercise for every single limiting belief you have. You don't have to do it all in one go. Just try to work on each limiting belief as it comes up naturally through the course of the day. Just make sure that you counteract them quickly by writing a positive affirmation for each one. You must also ensure that each affirmation is written in the present tense.

After writing the positive affirmations, you can burn the negative ideas and beliefs. Immerse the ashes in running water to ritually release them into the Universe. You will certainly feel lighter and more positive. You can retain the positive affirmations in either individual sheets or collect them in a journal that you keep with yourself at all times. Whenever the same negative thoughts come up, just refer to your journal to re-read and re-chant the affirmations you have created to counteract those thoughts.

FAITH IN ACTION

Action always speaks louder than words. The Universe can hear your innermost thoughts, and your actions tell the Universe what you truly feel inside your heart. If you are saying you are expecting to get that job in New Zealand and are looking forward to moving there in two months, but you settle for taking a job in your local city to feel safe, that's not faith in action.

When I was manifesting a healthy marriage, I cleared up one side of the closet and started laying out two plates every time I had a meal. I was living as if I was already married to my husband. In a few months, a chance meeting turned into the romance of a life-time. Similarly, when I wanted to move to a different city, I started packing my things well in advance, even before the move had become official.

I am not suggesting that you have to do something similar or go to any crazy extreme to prove to the Universe that you are truly ready to receive your manifestation. What you need is strong conviction and unflinching faith that what you want has already been granted to you. There may be a delay in receiving the order you have placed with the Universe, but it is yours and will show up at your door when the time is right. When you have this kind of conviction and faith, your actions will automatically become aligned with what you believe to be true.

EXERCISE

Review the manifestations you are currently working on and analyze whether your thoughts, actions, and emotions are fully aligned with what you want to receive or not. If not, then just continue practicing the visualizations and affirmations to induce the state of the wish fulfilled within your consciousness. There-after, drop the desire and get busy living your best life. At the same time, make sure the actions you take show that you have faith you will receive what you desire.

CHAPTER 9
LACK OF GRATITUDE

> If the only prayer you ever say in your entire life is thank you, it will be enough.

MEISTER ECKHART (BRAINYQUOTE, N.D.)

Gratitude is the most powerful form of prayer. Every time we feel thankful for what we have, we ask the Universe to bless us with more of the same. On the contrary, constantly complaining about a lack of something (both mentally or verbally) sends the wrong kind of message to the Universe. For the Universe, nothing is good or bad; there are only experiences, and you always get what you ask for. The Universe understands what you ask for by observing what you focus on. So, if you focus on the lack of something, then you ask for more of the same.

It's like attending a holiday dinner where you get served brussel sprouts amongst a host of other dishes that you actually like. You think you will finish the brussel sprouts first because you absolutely loathe those tiny leafy green balls. The hostess notices how quickly and determinedly you are finishing your brussel sprouts and serves you more of them. Before you know it, all you are eating is the thing you hate the most—brussel sprouts!

The Universe is your hostess, and by constantly thinking about how much you hate the house you are living in or the car you are driving, you are telling the Universe you want more of the same thing. The reason why people's lives don't change is because they remain stuck in a rut, blaming others, God, or the Universe. Most people don't know what they want. I know this because almost every time I have asked someone who was complaining about how much their life sucks, I also ask them what kind of life they want. They generally go speechless, not knowing how to react.

If you want the Universe to give you what you desire, then you must start feeling grateful for it as if you already have what you desire. You also need to start expressing gratitude for all the blessings that you already have in your life. I know there are some people in this world who would say there's nothing good in their life. That's just not possible; it is simply a perspective. It is human nature to not value what we have until we no longer have that thing. I am sure there are a lot of things in your life that someone else wishes they had. There are definitely many people in this world who believe they would be the happiest person in the world if they had your life. Look for things to be grateful for, and you'll find that there are innumerable blessings in your life.

EXERCISE: START AND END EACH DAY WITH GRATITUDE

If you want to completely change your life within the next twenty-one days, then you have to adopt a simple practice. As soon as you wake up, write down at least five things you are grateful for. They don't have to be big things; even the fact that you have a pen to write with is something worth being grateful for. Don't write the same things every day. Challenge yourself to write something new every single day. Nothing is too small or insignificant to be grateful for. In fact, the less you take your life and your body for granted, the more blessed your life becomes.

Do this exercise every morning immediately after getting out of bed. It will put you in a positive state of mind. You'll be better equipped to face whatever may come your way over the course of the day. However, you'll be surprised by how smoothly your days go by when you are in a positive frame of mind. Even when challenges come up, you must challenge yourself to be grateful for them, as they are opportunities for growth. The challenges are there to compel you to upgrade yourself to an even finer version of yourself.

In the evening, do the same exercise before retiring for the night, except that I would like you to write down five things that happened on that day that you are grateful for. Even on the most challenging of days, there is always something to be grateful for. This exercise will help you develop the habit of focusing on the positive in all circumstances. Your perspective is the most powerful thing in the world. By shifting your perspective, you can turn any challenge into a blessing.

Do this exercise morning and night for at least twenty-one days. Don't miss a single day. There has been a lot of research showing the fact that it takes at least twenty-one days to build a new habit. If you miss a single day or a single session (morning or evening), then start again from day one. Like most things in life, being grateful is a habit. It is a muscle that you develop and strengthen through practice. The more you practice, the better you get at it!

I am sure this exercise will be extremely transformative for you. At the end of the twenty-one-day period, if you feel your life has changed for the better (I am sure it will happen), then you can continue this exercise for the rest of your life. It should become a daily habit like brushing your teeth every morning and evening. Besides, if you can do this at the two most important times of the day, when the doorways of the subconscious are wide open, then it will also become easier for you to practice it throughout the day.

DON'T ENVY THOSE WHO HAVE WHAT YOU DESIRE

How do you feel when you see someone having the home, the career, the relationship, or the money you desire? Do you feel happy for them? Or do you start sinking deep into the quicksand of self-pity? I know it is not easy to give up on envy, but you must do it if you want to be successful with manifesting.

I am sure you have heard the saying that there is no "other" and that everyone else is a reflection of you. The world outside has always been a reflection of the world inside. Think about it; the world as we know it exists only when we observe it. When you close your eyes and sink into deep sleep, this world and everything in it ceases to exist, from your perspective.

It is also a scientific fact that all the things that appear to be solid in this world aren't solid at all. Every single thing in this vast Universe is in a state of vibration. If you were to zoom in on any object, the solidity of that object would dissolve until you reach a point where nothing but atoms in motion exist. It is very similar to how a computer image breaks down in pixels when you zoom in on the picture.

What you are experiencing in your life right now is the sum total of your thoughts and emotions. Nothing in your reality can exist without your permission. Due to our ignorance, we have manifested things, people, and circumstances that aren't aligned with our desires. It is in our hands to change that. No one can save you except for you. You are your own savior, and you are the creator of your own Universe.

Once you begin to understand these profound truths, it becomes easier to not envy others. You will realize the fact that whatever someone else is experiencing is the sum total of their thoughts, emotions, and beliefs. If you want what they have, then you can create it as well by simply changing your thoughts, emotions, and beliefs. Isn't that easier than allowing yourself to burn in the all-consuming fire of envy?

Besides, it is important to understand what envy is. Envy is a feeling arising from the desire for what someone else has. In a way, you feel the other person doesn't deserve what they have; you should have what they have instead. The problem with a feeling like this is what you wish for another is exactly what you wish for yourself.

The idea of the "other" is only an illusion of the mind. People may look and seem different to you, but every single person who comes into your energy field represents different aspects of your own self. Even the people you feel you have nothing in common with are mirroring you in one way or another.

What you see in others is also what you see in yourself. If you judge others harshly, then it is likely that you are judging yourself harshly as well. When you are loving toward yourself, then it also becomes easier to be loving toward others. You really can't ever treat another person better than you treat yourself, so the root of all transformation lies in changing yourself. This includes what you wish for others.

Every time you bless another person, you simultaneously bless yourself. The next time you see someone who has something you desire, see yourself merging with that person as if you and they were one (because you are) and let yourself feel all the happiness that you'd feel if you had what they have. If you can get yourself to feel happy for them, then you are sending a strong message to the Universe that you are ready to receive what they have. The Universe will definitely give the same thing to you. The windfall of good fortune often comes unexpectedly. Get in the habit of blessing others and feeling happy for their successes. The wheels of fortune will start turning in your favor sooner than you can imagine.

At the same time, keep in mind that every time you think to yourself that someone else doesn't deserve what they have, you are essentially telling the Universe that you don't deserve it as well. Be careful with your thoughts and emotions; just because no one in the world is hearing them doesn't mean the Universe isn't. Your internal dialogue is your communication with the Universe. You want it to be as positive and uplifting as possible.

GIVE UP THE SCARCITY MINDSET

At the root of envy lies the scarcity mindset. We don't think others should have what we desire because we erroneously hold on to the idea that what we want is only available in a limited supply. This can't be further from the truth. There is abundance in the Universe for everyone. There is enough room for everyone to be amazing and for every single person to have exactly what they desire.

Thanks to the conditioning we have received from family, teachers, and society, we have started to believe that there is only so much available to go around for everyone. We hear things like the 99 percent are poor only because the 1 percent are hogging all the wealth of the world. From a very gross material perspective, one may think this is true, but if you understand the principles of the spiritual realm, then you'll realize that there is no truth in such ideas or statements.

Every single thing in this world is made up of energy. Since there is an infinite and unlimited supply of energy, the same is true for all the things that are made up of that same energy. Our experience of scarcity stems from our own ignorance. Each one of us is a queen or a king, but our ignorance turns us into paupers who start believing that the things we want are too far out of reach.

Let me say this to you one more time: you can have, be, and do anything you want. Limitations are present only in your mind; the Universe has no limits. All things are possible for the Universe! Another person getting what you desire is proof that what you want can be yours. If they can have it, then so can you.

You simply need to shift your perspective to see that other people having what you desire is not something worth envying but something worth celebrating. They are you, and you are them. What they have is also yours. It's just that your order is on its way while theirs has arrived at their doorstep. Bless them, partake in their happiness, and celebrate their success. After all, they are showing you what's possible for you as well!

EXERCISE

Write down the limiting beliefs that are currently governing your life. Statements like "I am never going to get married," "I will never be rich," "Thanks to all the oppression in this world, I am never going to succeed," and "It is impossible to succeed in this kind of an economy." These are just some examples of the kind of statements that may be holding you back.

Once you have written everything down, take another sheet of paper and create a positive affirmation to counteract each one of those statements and beliefs. Once you have written down the new affirmations, burn the sheet where you had written your negative beliefs. Discard the ashes in a body of running water and feel the release. Whenever those limiting beliefs start coming up again and you find yourself slipping into the dungeon of negativity, pull out the sheet with the positive affirmations and start reading them (out aloud or silently in your mind).

BLESS EVERY PERSON YOU MEET

There's a lot of truth to the saying whatever we give away comes back to us multiplied. A person who is constantly finding faults in others receives the same analysis of their own faults back in kind. If you gossip about others, then it is inevitable that others will also gossip about you. Similarly, kindness attracts greater kindness. It may not immediately come back from the person you are being kind to, but it will definitely come back from one source or another.

From now on, get in the habit of blessing others. Start focusing on the good in others. There is always something worth appreciating in every single person. Become a diamond miner, the type of person who always finds something good in every person and in every situation. The Universe will reward you handsomely by showering you with greater blessings than you have ever deemed possible. Trust me on that and just give it a try!

CHAPTER 10
NOT BEING CAREFUL WITH YOUR MENTAL AND SPIRITUAL DIET

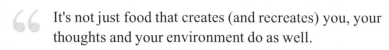 It's not just food that creates (and recreates) you, your thoughts and your environment do as well.

MICHAEL CORTHELL (GOODREADS, N.D.)

Your diet isn't just what you eat. It is also the thoughts you allow into your energy field and the emotions you let yourself feel. Just like your physical body is made out of the food you eat, your life is the sum total of all the thoughts, emotions, and feelings you have ever experienced.

Very much like how one night of pizza-hogging and beer-guzzling can ruin all the progress you have made that week, one bad thought can ruin the mental and spiritual equilibrium you have acquired by working hard on yourself for a while, especially if you allow that one thought to suck you into a whirlpool of negativity.

We are often tempted to indulge in darkness or negativity. For example, the allure of reading in the news exactly how the murder took place or the temptation to say something nasty about the co-worker we aren't too fond of. Darkness is constantly pulling us in its direction. It is quite simply an essential part of the human experience. The only way you can counteract it is by practicing spiritual discipline. You have to say no each time.

Just because you have managed to consistently say no for a significant amount of time doesn't mean that you will be safe today or tomorrow. At any point, you can fall, though it is okay (and normal) to fall once in a while. Instead of wallowing in guilt and self-loathing, every time that happens, you must simply brush off your knees and get back up. Resilience is the key here. Besides, the more often you practice spiritual discipline, the easier it gets over time.

GUARD THE DOORWAYS OF YOUR SUBCONSCIOUS MIND

By now, you already know that it is your subconscious mind that dictates your experience of reality. Every single experience of life has emerged out of a belief or idea that you carry in your subconscious mind. Your outer reality is always a carbon copy of your inner reality. Hence, if you want to change your outer reality, then you must begin by altering your inner reality.

 You are the sum total of everything you've ever seen, heard, eaten, smelled, been told, forgotten—it's all there. Everything influences each of us, and because of that I try to make sure that my experiences are positive.

MAYA ANGELOU (GOODREADS, N.D.)

As I shared earlier, the two most important times of the day are mornings (immediately after rising) and evenings (right before you fall asleep). At these two times of the day, the doorways of your subconscious become wide open. Whatever you allow into your energy field at these two times will easily sink into the deepest layers of your subconscious mind.

Don't waste this time watching television or movies or sulking about how bad everything in your life is. There's a reason why you get such bad sleep every time you fall asleep watching a horror film! You are allowing that horror on the screen to become part of your reality. It shouldn't be surprising that you feel fearful and negative throughout the night, perhaps also the next morning, and over the next few days.

When you fall asleep feeling miserable and negative, you are allowing more such events to occur in the future that leave you feeling miserable and negative. By using these two times of the day intentionally, you can rewire your subconscious mind, thereby altering your "reality." You must use these two times of the day for practicing visualizations, affirmations, and meditation. It will help with impressing the subconscious mind positively, and the results will manifest into your physical reality sooner rather than later.

Also, if you are someone who falls asleep listening to music, then you must become very selective about the kind of music you are listening to. Even when you think you are sleeping, your subconscious mind is wide awake. It is observing and absorbing everything in your environment like a sponge. This is why I strongly advise against falling asleep with the news playing in the background. Most of what is shared as "news" on television is every-thing bad that has happened on a given day in the world. If you fall asleep listening to such things every night, you are making room for such things to manifest in your reality. I'm not suggesting that you give up on watching the news altogether; just don't do it early in the morning right after you get out of bed or at night right before you fall asleep.

To be honest, I gave up on watching "news" altogether a long time ago. I don't feel like I miss out on much as I always get the important updates from the people close to me. I started feeling more at peace with myself and my life when I stopped watching the news. You have to use your own discretion here. Perhaps staying updated with current affairs is part of your work profile. Just be careful with how much of this information you are watching or reading. Try to limit your consumption of news to only what is essential for you to know and do it at a time of the day when the subconscious mind is less impressionable, like in the afternoon or early evening.

Keep in mind that every time you allow yourself to feel or imagine something vividly, you are making an impression on the subconscious mind. It is bound to affect your experience of life in one way or another. Yes, what you are imagining may not manifest if the impression is weak but you never know. There have been times when I thought about something only once or twice and it happened. The best way to counteract such negative thoughts and images is by imagining the exact opposite immediately. So every time you find yourself thinking or imagining what you don't want, counteract it by thinking and imagining exactly what you want.

Stay away from consuming any content that leaves you feeling ill at ease. The feeling in your gut often tells you exactly what is good for you and what is not. Don't read books or magazines that bog you down. Instead, read those books and magazines that empower you. In fact, reading is an excellent habit that can rewire your subconscious mind with more positive thoughts and beliefs. But of course, be very careful with what kind of content you are consuming. Invest in good books that can help you become a better person. I personally like to read multiple books at a time. I focus on reading those books that can help me tackle a challenge I am facing or that can help me get ahead in a particular area of life that is important to me at the time.

A good book is like a good friend who empowers you with knowledge and wisdom that can help you become a better person. You must exercise the same kind of discretion while picking which articles to read online or in printed magazines. You have to also be careful with which social media accounts you follow online and how they make you feel. Follow only those accounts that truly inspire you. Use them to visualize the life you want to live.

Many people think that social media is something toxic that must be done away with altogether. I beg to differ. I believe it is a tool just like the knives in your kitchen. A chef can use the knives to carve gourmet food while a murderer can use the same tool to butcher another human being. The problem is not with the tool but with the person using the tool. You can use social media as a tool for inspiration when you are intentional and careful about the kind of content you are consuming.

It is also very important to get against feelings of envy and jealousy while browsing through other people's social media posts. Never forget that you are watching the highlight reel of someone else's life. You are seeing what they want you to see. It's not their entire life. You don't know what they may have been through to get where they currently are in life. Besides, as I shared in the previous chapter, every time you see someone who has what you desire for yourself, bless them. This way, you'd be blessing yourself as well. Take it as an example that if it is possible for them, then it is also possible for you. Be grateful they are showing you that what you want truly does exist and is within your grasp as well. To have anything in life or to be anyone you want to be, you simply need to convince your subconscious mind that you can have, be, or do what you desire.

WHO ARE YOU SPENDING TIME WITH?

One of the greatest motivational speakers of all time, Jim Rohn, once famously said, "You are the average of the five people you spend the most time with" (Goodreads, n.d.). Indeed, we are all strongly influenced by the company we keep, not just in terms of our habits and behavior but also spiritually.

Spend a day with someone who is bitter and negative, you'll end up feeling drained by the end of the day. There is an energy exchange constantly going on in this world. A person who is bitter and negative vibrates at a low frequency. When you come in contact with their energy field and you are a much more positive person, it may cause energy to flow to them from you. This is why we begin feeling drained after being around a negative person.

The important thing here is to learn how to protect your energy. Whenever I interact with someone who has a negative mindset, I imagine a ball of pink light entering my body and flooding every inch of it. I imagine this ball of light surrounding me so that my entire physical and energy body is engulfed by it. Thereafter, I imagine a layer of electric blue life surrounding this ball of pink light. I say a silent prayer or affirmation: "Whatever negative vibrations may be coming toward me shall bounce back and go to the Universe where they will be transformed."

This is a very powerful practice. It really works! You can use it to seal your aura and energy field. Also, I'm not suggesting that you begin fearing every person you come across simply because of whatever negative vibrations they may be emitting. Your goal should be to become so positive that the other person feels empowered by it instead of you getting depleted by their negativity. Trust me, each one of us is constantly influencing other people's energy fields just as much as they are influencing ours. It's always the person with the stronger energy field who ends up influencing the other one. You have to always choose to be the person with the stronger, more positive energy field. This way, whoever comes into your energy field will either be transformed or get repelled.

The more positive you become, the more you'll realize that the people around you are also changing for the better, or else they will disappear from your life without a trace. This is because those who are ready to be transformed make the choice to be better, whether consciously or subconsciously. Anyone who resists change will get repelled from your energy field and will gravitate toward people who are vibrating at a similar vibrational frequency to them.

Many of my old friendships faded as I progressed further on

this journey of improving myself and my life. This is a natural process, and you should not resist it. Always remember that the Universe abhors a vacuum; every time you lose something, you are making room for something new and better to manifest in your life. There are no exceptions to the rule. If some relationships fade away as you move forward on this journey, trust that new more beautiful relationships will manifest in your life.

Another thing I want you to understand is that the people we surround ourselves with often indicate to us where we currently are in life. There is nothing coincidental about the circle we belong to at any stage of life because we always surround ourselves with people who are similar to us. For instance, an alcoholic will be friends with other alcoholics, a millionaire will be friends with other millionaires, and so on.

You have to understand that most people want to live in their comfort zones. They fear change and prefer to take the path of least resistance in all circumstances. Hence, every time you start doing something to change your life, it makes other people very uncom- fortable. It happened with me, and it happens with every single person who tries to change their life for the better. People get trig- gered by it because of what it says about themselves.

Let's say you have spent your whole life around people who have unhealthy eating habits. They love you and cheer for you as long as you are participating in their unhealthy food fests. The moment you announce that you have decided to stop eating junk food and become a regular at the gym, they'll try to sabotage you, whether consciously or subconsciously.

It's not like they are bad people or are intentionally trying to harm you, or that they don't want you to have a better life. They react the way they do because you are making them uncomfortable about their own choices. They know their way of life isn't right—it doesn't feel right deep inside their gut—but they are not willing to do the work to change their own life. It is easier to continue to surround themselves with other people who have chosen the same way of life. That in turn helps them validate their own choices. You have to let such friendships and relationships go. It is not worth dimming your own light just to make others feel comfortable with their darkness.

We have all come into this world to grow and become the highest version of ourselves. Every person has their own unique journey. It is not worth giving up on our own journey just to fit in with others. Trust that every time an old relationship fades away, a new one will take its place.

I know this can be especially difficult to contend with in the case of close family. You don't have to cut your close family members who are negative completely out of your life. Just limit your interactions with them and establish strong boundaries by telling them that you'd rather not discuss certain topics with them. Reassure them that you love them and respect their choices but that you'd appreciate it if they would also respect yours. When you spend time with them, focus on the things you have in common with them instead of putting all your attention on the differences.

EXERCISE

Create a list of five or more people in your life who inspire you and like whom you want to be. Start spending more time with these people. If they are people you know in person, then figure out how you can spend more time in their physical presence. In case it is a famous person, you can read books by and about them, watch their videos, or listen to their audios. Observe their habits, mindset, and ways of thinking. Try to absorb and inculcate them into your own consciousness.

Every time you must interact with someone who is negative, practice the aura protection exercise I described in the last section of this chapter.

CHAPTER 11
DISCUSSING YOUR MANIFESTATION WITH OTHERS

> At a stage in life, you learn to talk less. That is, let your work do the talking. Hence, work hard in silence. The evidence will be clear for all to see.

OSCAR BIMPONG (GOODREADS, N.D.)

I know just how tempting it is to want to tell others, especially those closest to us, what we expect to receive from the Universe. If, like me, you have made the mistake of sharing your excitement with others prematurely, then you already know how it usually pans out. You are met with doubt, suspicion, and all kinds of other emotions.

The thing you need to understand is that we have all come into this world on a unique journey. Just because we have been born amongst certain people we call family doesn't mean that they will be similar to us or that their journey will have much in common with ours. This life is a very brief experience in the infinity of time. Our loved ones are the co-passengers with whom we share the train compartment of this life's journey. There will come a point when they will get off the train at their own destination. We may be headed to a completely different destination than they are.

The most important life skill I have taught myself is the art of not taking things personally. You have to realize that, as human beings, we are inherently self-absorbed; that's just the nature of the human psyche. We are always thinking about ourselves and how things impact us. Our understanding of the world is defined by our personal relationship with the world.

The greatest gift you can give yourself is to develop this understanding that, most of the time, other people's words and behavior toward you has nothing to do with you. People are usually projecting their limitations and beliefs onto you. This is why I am a strong believer of moving in silence. Don't tell others what you are trying to manifest, as they may unwittingly sabotage your efforts.

It's not like the people in your life don't want the best for you. They are just shackled by their own conditioning and limitations. They believe they can't do certain things, that some things are impossible for them. They will project those limitations and beliefs onto you to try to convince you that you can't have what you desire.

One of my favorite scenes from the movie *Pursuit of Happiness* is when Will Smith's character tells his son, "Don't ever let someone tell you, you can't do something. Not even me. You got a dream, you got to protect it. People can't do something themselves, they want to tell you you can't do it. You want something, go get it. Period."

There is a lot of wisdom in this advice. People are seldom telling you the truth about you; they are simply projecting their beliefs about themselves onto you. Don't ever let someone else's limited thinking and imagination dictate your reality. Therefore, it is always best to keep your manifestations private.

HOW YOUR MANIFESTATIONS MAY BE GETTING SABOTAGED

Now, what if the other person isn't saying anything negative about themselves or you. Is it okay to share your manifestation with them in that case?

Every time I have shared my manifestation with others, I have felt something happen at the spiritual level. It was as if, the moment I shared what I was trying to manifest with someone else, that manifestation was sabotaged, even if the other person did not say anything negative verbally.

I feel the way it works is that a new manifestation is like a delicate plant that we nurture and water with our imagination. Just like a tiny plant that has begun to sprout must be protected from the harsh elements of the environment, we must protect our manifestations from any form of negative energy. It is hard enough to keep ourselves positive; why make things harder by getting other people's energy entangled in our manifestations! Our loved ones want the best for us, but they may have certain limiting beliefs that they can project onto you energetically, even if they don't do so verbally.

Another reason why I'm not in favor of sharing your manifestation before it has come to pass is because loved ones often begin to put a lot of pressure on you. For instance, let's say you are dating someone while you are trying to manifest a marriage with the right person. You share what you are trying to manifest with your parents, and now every week when you see them, they ask you if things have moved forward in your relationship or not.

Obviously, they want the best for you and their intention is to see you happy, but such questions cause frustration in our psyche. Also, in the example above, the person you are dating may not even be the right person for you to marry. You are trying to manifest a marriage with the right person, but the right person may or may not be the person you are currently dating. But since your parents can see you are already in a relationship, they may start pressuring you to turn that relationship into a marriage, since you have expressed to them a desire to get married.

FEAR OF FAILURE

Let's say that the person or people you share your manifestation with are fully supportive. They have no limiting beliefs with regards to your manifestation, and they truly believe you can get what you want. There's another thing that may happen the moment you share your manifestation with others. It has happened to me, and I am quite sure you'll be able to relate to it.

The moment you share your manifestation with another person, you start feeling a strong fear of failure. It's like now that you've told someone about it, you must turn your manifestation into a reality; otherwise, you'll be letting another person down along with yourself. This can make you impatient and even obsessive as you start to try hard to manipulate the outcome you desire.

Once again, this proves that keeping your manifestations private is the best strategy. It is hard enough to manage your own expectations around it, let alone having to manage another person's expectations along with yours! Why make things unnecessarily more complicated for yourself? If you weigh the pros and cons of sharing your manifestations with others, then it is quite clear that the negatives outweigh the benefits. It is more harmful than it can be beneficial. I personally don't think it is beneficial at all.

Of course, there may be situations where you have to share something related to your manifestation with others, especially if you need their participation to move things forward. You can share those things that have already come to pass, but practice the discipline to keep to yourself the end goal you have in sight. For instance, if you are manifesting a successful business, then you may have to share with your family your intentions for starting a business. However, you don't have to tell them how you see it becoming a multi-million dollar brand at some point.

You can and should share your happiness with others once you have successfully manifested what you desire. It is a lot more rewarding to discuss your manifestation when you have the result in front of you and no one will question your ability to get it, and you will not be gripped by the fear of disappointing them once you achieve what you said you wanted to achieve.

There is also something really satisfying about building in silence and then letting everyone be surprised by your success. When you need others to support you on your journey, ask them for their assistance as you are moving forward one step at a time. Avoid telling them the exact dream you have and the vision you are holding on to.

EXCEPTIONS TO THIS RULE

There are certain exceptions to this rule. You can share your vision with another person when you collaborate with them to manifest the same dream together. For instance, let's say you and your spouse want to manifest a beautiful home. You have both discussed at length exactly what kind of house you see yourself living in. In this case, it is perfectly fine for you to share what you want to manifest with your spouse as you are both operating as a joint unit. You are one. But you both must still resist the urge to share your manifestation with anyone outside your circle of two.

In another situation, perhaps you are the owner of a company and are trying to manifest a specific turnover. You can get together with your staff and teach them how to visualize the outcome you desire. In such cases, the power of your joint efforts can help strengthen the manifestation.

Keep in mind that even in these cases, you are still traversing the landscape of your imagination alone. You still have to have your own imaginal act to get into the state of the wish fulfilled. Other people have to draft their own imaginal act to enter the state of the wish fulfilled as their imaginal act needs to be emotionally evocative to them.

BE CAREFUL WHO YOU SHARE THE GOOD NEWS WITH

Even after your manifestation has come to pass, you will want to exercise a lot of discretion in who you share the good news with. Some people will be genuinely happy for you, while others may envy you. And there may be others yet who will act like a wet blanket.

I remember running to my grandmother after school, wanting to show her how well I had performed on a test. Instead of reveling in my success, she said something like, "Are you sure the teacher graded your paper correctly?"

This dampened all my enthusiasm and excitement about my success. I began to doubt if my success was real and, worse still, if I even deserved it. Only as an adult did I come to realize that she was projecting her own fears and insecurities onto me. She did not believe that good things could happen to her. Hence, if she saw anyone in her circle celebrating any good news, she had to project her own lack of success onto them. It's not like she was a bad person or anything; she simply had not done the work to undo her conditioning. She also did not know how to create the life she wanted, if she even knew exactly what it was she wanted. She lived in her comfort zone, which unfortunately was a place of negativity and a lack of faith in anything good happening to her.

I'm not suggesting that you cut negative people out of your life; just become more selective about what you share with them. You can have a beautiful relationship with others without sharing every single part of your life with them. Make sure you share your good news with people who would be genuinely happy for you.

Of course, for any major success that you achieve, the results will be visible to everyone. In that case, you just have to ignore any negativity that wet blankets or haters try projecting onto you. Let their words come and go. Don't pay any attention to them. It is easier to not invest any emotional energy into someone else's negativity when you realize that they are projecting their own insecurities and limiting beliefs onto you. What they are saying isn't about you; it is about them.

EXERCISE

Create a list of people who you know genuinely want the best for you and vow to celebrate your success with them. Of course, if you are in a position of authority in an organization or you are a public figure with a following, you can share it with your tribe. Just become selective with whom you include in your closest circle, as those people influence your energy just as much as they are influenced by yours.

FINAL WORDS

Thank you for picking up this book and trusting me to guide you with your manifestations. I hope this book gives you the results you desire. If you haven't put into practice everything you have read in this book, I would suggest you go back to Chapter 1 and start practicing what I have shared with you. Always remember that practice makes perfect. As with anything in life, you get better at manifesting by regularly practicing the principles that govern it.

Manifesting is a science as much as it is an art. If you follow my methods and avoid the pitfalls discussed in the book, then you will definitely get the results. The entire Universe is made out of energy. The million dollar mansions we admire are made out of the same energy as a shack by the side of the street. What you believe you deserve and what you truly expect to receive is exactly what the Universe will deliver to you. Why not believe that you can receive things beyond your wildest dreams?

If there is anyone in this world who has what you desire, then that's proof that what you want is possible. It's possible for a person to have the thing or be the person you desire to have or be. If it can happen for them, then why can't it happen for you? If you dig deep into their life and their psyche, you'll realize that the only difference between them and you is what they believe to be true for themselves and their life. They believe they are worthy and deserving of what they have; that's why they have manifested the reality they are living. You can do it too.

You don't need money, talent, or connections to manifest anything in this world. You simply need to make a choice in your own mind that you already have what you desire. Once you plant that idea into your subconscious mind, the Universe will turn the world upside down to bring you what you desire. Whatever money, connections, talent, skills, or anything else you may require in this world will come to you of its own accord. You just need to imagine and enter the state of the wish fulfilled. And when the Universe prompts you to take certain actions, only then will you take inspired action.

Sit back and relax. Let the Universe work on your behalf. You deserve to have, be, and do everything you desire. It's all possible, and it's all coming to you much faster than you realize!

Love,

Mia Hammond

Leave a 1-Click Review!

Customer Reviews

⭐⭐⭐⭐⭐ 2

5.0 out of 5 stars ▾

5 star		100%	Share your thoughts with other customers
4 star		0%	
3 star		0%	Write a customer review
2 star		0%	
1 star		0%	

See all verified purchase reviews ▸

If you enjoyed this book, I would be incredibly thankful if you could take 60 seconds to write a brief review on Amazon, even if just a few sentences. Thank you!

https://www.amazon.com/Why-You-Attracting-What-Want-ebook/dp/B0B2PMX97Z/review

Other Books You'll Love!

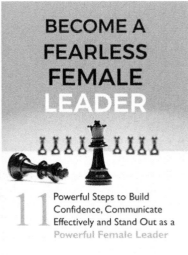

REFERENCES

Angelou, M. (n.d.). Goodreads. Retrieved May 16, 2022, from https://www.goodreads.com/quotes/1227209-you-are-the-sum-total-of-everything-you-ve-ever-seen

Bach, R. (n.d.). BrainyQuote. Retrieved May 16, 2022, from https://www.brainyquote.com/quotes/richard_bach_383522

Bimpong, O. (n.d.). Goodreads. Retrieved May 16, 2022, from https://www.goodreads.com/quotes/tag/talk-less

Canfield, J. (n.d.). Goodreads. Retrieved May 16, 2022, from https://www.goodreads.com/quotes/495741-everything-you-want-is-on-the-other-side-of-fear

Corthell, M. (n.d.). Goodreads. Retrieved May 16, 2022, from https://www.goodreads.com/quotes/tag/you-are-what-you-eat

Eckhart, M. (n.d.). BrainyQuote. Retrieved May 16, 2022, from https://www.brainyquote.com/quotes/meister_eckhart_149158

Emerson, R. W. (n.d.). passiton.com. Retrieved May 16, 2022, from https://www.passiton.com/inspirational-quotes/3392-what- lies-behind-us-and-what-lies-before-us

Goddard, N. (2018). *Your Faith is Your Fortune.* Merchant Books.

Goddard, N. (2020). *The Neville Collection: All 10 Books by a Modern Master.* Independently published.

Hebrews 11:1 - King James Version. Bible Gateway. (n.d.). Retrieved May 16, 2022, from https://www.biblegateway.com/passage/?search=Hebrews+11%3A1&version=KJV

Hicks, E., & Hicks, J. (2004). *Ask and It Is Given: Learning to Manifest Your Desires.* Hay House Inc.

Hill, N. (2005). *Think and Grow Rich.* Jeremy P. Tarcher/Penguin.

Lee, B. (n.d.). The Minds Journal. Retrieved May 16, 2022, from https://themindsjournal.com/i-am-two-of-most-powerful-words/

Proctor, B. (1997). *You were born rich.* LifeSuccess Productions.

Rohn, J. (n.d.). Goodreads. Retrieved May 16, 2022, from https://www.goodreads.com/quotes/1798-you-are-the-average-of-the-five-people-you-spend

Stowe, H. B. (n.d.). BrainyQuote. Retrieved May 16, 2022, from https://www.brainyquote.com/quotes/harriet_beecher_stowe_117728

Watts, A. W. (n.d.). Goodreads. Retrieved May 18, 2022, from https://www.goodreads.com/quotes/tag/illusion

Printed in Great Britain
by Amazon

23680141R00067